WALKING

Rediscovering

A SACRED

the Labyrinth as

PATH

a Spiritual Tool

Dr. Lauren Artress

Riverhead Books
New York

Riverhead Books
Published by The Berkley Publishing Group
A division of Penguin Putnam Inc.
375 Hudson Street
New York, New York 10014

Copyright © 1995 by Lauren Artress
Book design by Richard Oriolo
Cover design by Isabella Fasciano

First Riverhead hardcover edition: May 1995
First Riverhead trade paperback edition: June 1996
Riverhead trade paperback ISBN: 1-57322-547-9

The Penguin Putnam Inc. World Wide Web site address is
http://www.penguinputnam.com

The Library of Congress has catalogued the Riverhead hardcover
edition as follows:

Artress, Lauren.
Walking a sacred path : rediscovering the labyrinth as a spiritual
tool / Lauren Artress.
    p. cm.
  Includes bibliographical references.
  ISBN 1-57322-007-8 (alk. paper)
  1. Labyrinths—Religious aspects. 2. Meditations. 3. Spiritual
life. I. Title.
BL325.L.3A77 1995   95-3435 CIP
  291.3'7—dc20

Printed in the United States of America

20   19

Contents

A c k n o w l e d g m e n t s

I want to thank Alan Jones, dean of Grace Cathedral, for his support even when we both thought the idea of walking the labyrinth was odd at best. Thank you to the trustees, staff, and congregation of Grace Cathedral, especially the men's and women's groups who donated money to create the canvas labyrinth. Thank you to the many people who made the labyrinth floor tapestry a reality. To Gilda Iriarte, who headed me in the right direction way back when, to Jan Johnson, my friend and luckily my editor, Susan Petersen and Wendy Carlton, my publishers at Riverhead, Gloria Karpinski, Jim Strong, Judith Cornell, Andrew Harvey, Maggie Kent, Therese Quinlan, who ably serves as the Quest program manager, and the many, many labyrinth volunteers who came forward to help. Special thanks to Barbara Hartford for her love and nurturance of me and the Labyrinth Project.

INTRODUCTION

We can discern . . . a transformation of human personality in progress which is of evolutionary proportions, a shift of consciousness fully as epochmaking as the appearance of speech or of the tool making talents in our cultural repertory.

—Theodore Roszak

I grew up in rural northern Ohio along the Chagrin River. Chagrin is a Native American word for clear. In the summertime, long rapids bubbled with cold, fresh water. Because it was purified by the sun, we even trusted the water to drink. Our home sat atop a thirty-five-foot cliff overlooking the river. Across the river trees covered the hill. Upstream the contours of the hillside grew into a huge shale cliff topped with more trees. The flat top of that cliff was my spiritual home. I spent hours walking and reflecting there, feeling at one with nature and the mystery that invisibly weaves in and through all life.

In seventh grade, the world began to open up to me. Its beauty and its intrigue moved me. One summer day I waded knee-deep through the rapids across the river. I climbed the ravine and wound my way up the trail to the top of a two-hundred-foot cliff, majestically wooded and silent. As I walked along the cliff's edge, something caught my eye. Flashes of light—like mirrors reflecting sunlight—came from the river far below. When I focused my long-distance sight into the water, I realized that the flashes were the sun reflecting off the sides of fish swimming in a school. These forty to fifty small fish, called "shiners," were swimming in formation. First they were a rectangle, swimming in one direction for several yards. Then, in a flash, they turned and swam back in the opposite direction. In another flash, they formed a circle rotating around an invisible center. Then, flash, they broke that formation to form themselves anew.

Dusk surprised me and forced me to descend the trail and cross the river to home. I knew that I had stumbled onto something that held great mystery. But I had no name for it, no way of understanding it. Years later I learned that the Native Americans call what I witnessed the "dance of the fishes." I had stumbled onto a dance, a sacred ritual, a divine secret: there are invisible patterns throughout all of nature and these patterns are imprinted within each species. The migration patterns of whales, the hibernation of bears, the mating dance of birds are all woven into the web of creation. So, too, is the longing within the human heart to love and nurture, to create, and to discover the mystery we live within and that lives within us.

Little did I know that this would be the first, of many encounters with sacred pattern in my life. This book is about the sacred pattern of the labyrinth, an ancient mystical tool that can help us prepare ourselves for the "transformation of human personality in progress" and accomplish a "shift in consciousness" as we seek spiritual maturity as a species. We are called to do nothing less.

In 1986, I was asked to serve as Canon Pastor of Grace Cathedral in San Francisco. Two years later we secured grant money and, with full support of the dean, Alan Jones, created a center called Quest: Grace Cathedral Center for Spiritual Wholeness. Quest's goal is to address the spiritual hunger in this country by building a bridge of understanding between the traditional church and the nontraditional forms of spirituality that are springing up in our culture.

One of the most astonishing events of my life was about to happen. It took me back into sacred pattern in a way I never expected. During a retreat, I stumbled across an ancient mystical tool called the labyrinth, which had dropped out of human awareness more than 350 years ago. I first began to research the labyrinth and then later introduced it to people at Grace Cathedral and in workshops around the country. I moved from curiosity to skepticism to profound respect for the uncanny gifts of insight, wisdom, and peace the labyrinth offers. It connects us to the depths of our souls so we can remember who we are.

Before I go further, I want to say that my work with the labyrinth, including my research into history and sacred geometry, aims to integrate people's psyche and soul. I am not a historian; I am a priest and a psychotherapist. My fundamental working question or principle has always been: How do I help people, including myself, to change?

Labyrinths are usually in the form of a circle

with a meandering but purposeful path, from the edge to the center and back out again, large enough to be walked into. Each has only one path, and once we make the choice to enter it, the path becomes a metaphor for our journey through life, sending us to the center of the labyrinth and then back out to the edge on the same path. The labyrinth is a spiritual tool meant to awaken us to the deep rhythm that unites us to ourselves and to the Light that calls from within. In surrendering to the winding path, the soul finds healing and wholeness.

The labyrinth that is the focus of this book is the classical eleven-circuit labyrinth. The best known example of this labyrinth remains embedded in the floor of Chartres Cathedral in France. The labyrinth in Grace Cathedral is modeled on the Chartres labyrinth. Since the end of 1991, when we first presented the labyrinth in the cathedral, at least two hundred thousand people have walked the approximately one-third-mile winding path. We've stopped counting.

Based on the circle, the universal symbol for unity and wholeness, the labyrinth sparks the human imagination and introduces it to a kaleidoscopic patterning that builds a sense of relationship: one person to another, to another, to many people, to creation of the whole. It enlivens the intuitive part of our nature and stirs within the human heart the longing for connectedness and the remembrance of our purpose for living.

The labyrinth is a sacred place and can give us firsthand experiences of the Divine. Please give yourself the gift of suspending your usual patterns of belief and judgment while you read *Walking a Sacred Path*. The labyrinth captures the essence of the medieval reality: a highly sensate world that was not plagued with so many splits between reason and imagination, thought and feeling, psyche and spirit. Be patient. This new territory may seem foreign at first.

I feel deeply honored to be working with this magnificent tool and want to encourage you to walk it for yourself at some time before the end of this century. Do not let others judge for you. Do not allow another person's uninformed opinion to dictate whether you walk the labyrinth. If, after you walk it, you do not feel drawn to it, take what you can and leave the rest. It is truly a pleasure and privilege to share the labyrinth with you.

Walking a
Sacred Path

O n e

TO WALK A
SACRED PATH

The great need of our time is for people to be
connected to spirit; for people to be connected to a core
of feeling in themselves that makes their lives vital and
full of meaning, that makes life a mystery ever-
more to be uncovered.

—Harold Stone
Sandplay

E arly in January 1991, I was in the midst of a
transition. Although I enjoyed my role as
Canon Pastor at Grace Cathedral, after five years I
was exhausted by its demands. I had been invited to
serve as Canon for Special Ministries and to continue to direct Quest, Grace Cathedral Center for
Spiritual Wholeness in San Francisco. In preparation, I needed time to go inward and attend to my

restless uncertainty. I decided to return to a Mystery School seminar with Dr. Jean Houston, an internationally known psychologist, scholar, and author whom I studied with in 1985.

Here I first encountered the labyrinth. In presenting this little-known medieval pattern, Jean described a powerful spiritual tool whose path would lead each of us to our own center. My interest was piqued. I lined up with the hundred or so other participants to walk the forty-foot-wide circular pattern taped to the floor. I was hardly prepared for the force of my own reaction. As soon as I set foot into the labyrinth I was overcome with an almost violent anxiety. Some part of me seemed to know that in this ancient and mysterious archetype, I was encountering something that would change the course of my life.

That evening, I felt drawn back to walk the labyrinth alone three more times. As my feet became surer of their way, my mind began to quiet. Walking, running, moving through the winding pathways as my instincts dictated, I felt joyous one minute, burdened the next. I seemed to step beyond time to where each moment stood triumphant in its own right.

Returning up the snowy hill to my cabin that night, I wondered what response the encounter with the labyrinth would elicit from my unconscious. I got my answer the next morning when I awoke, distressed from a dream of having had a heart attack. Was it a warning? Why this particular dream so close on the heels of my labyrinth walk? As I pondered the dream, I thought back to my father's heart attack. He had received a book from a friend called *Thank God for My Heart Attack*. The book described the challenge posed by a life-threatening event: to redesign your life so that it fits you instead of your attempting to fit into it.

The dream signaled to me that my life was going to change. Though I did not know it at the time, the labyrinth would help me bring more of myself to my work, to exercise my heart muscle as never before. I had connected with a sacred archetypal form that would lead me to do things I never imagined doing. It would lead me to places I had never imagined. Such is the power of the labyrinth.

After my initial experience, I knew I was to work with the labyrinth. Just what to do with it puzzled me until about three months later. I was literally walking in circles around my living room when it finally dawned on me: put the labyrinth in the sacred space of Grace Cathedral. When I first told a colleague about putting a labyrinth in the nave of the cathedral, I found my face turning red. But the idea would not leave me.

My reading about labyrinths got me through this early skepticism and uncertainty. I began to realize the profound need we all have to connect to the Spirit that enlivens us. We need that core feeling of connection to the Divine to give our lives meaning, to find the vision for the future. We need to awaken to a vision of a thriving, healthy planet that supports life among diverse communities. To evoke our vision, we need the experiences of archetypes that help us grasp the experience of unity and wholeness. The labyrinth is an archetype of wholeness, a sacred place that helps us rediscover the depths of our souls.

Two pieces of research needed to be complete before I could move ahead with the plan for a labyrinth in Grace Cathedral. I needed to go to Chartres Cathedral and experience the labyrinth, long held in obscurity, to find out for myself the depth of its potential. Second, I needed to meet with Keith Critchlow, a renowned British architect, who came to my attention through his article *Chartres Maze, A Model of the Universe?* Dr. Critchlow was teaching that summer at the Royal School of Architects at Oxford. My friend Barbara Hartford, a congregation member and trustee of the cathedral, agreed to travel with me. We packed two cameras, tape measures, and notepads for our research.

My first glimpse of Chartres Cathedral remains a distinct memory. It stands majestically on a hillside among miles of wheat fields. At a distance, there is no hint of the city that lies below its awesome presence. The cathedral was built on the highest sacred ground available, most likely following a long line of spiritual traditions. Once we saw the cathedral, it took almost an entire half-hour to drive up to it. To finally walk through the huge doors into this dark and wondrous monument was one of the highlights of my life.

We met Alan Jones, the dean of Grace Cathedral, his wife, Josephine, and two other congregation members and discussed the next morning's approach. The Chartres labyrinth is approximately forty-two feet in diameter, inlaid in the stone floor. It is barely recognizable, since it is usually covered with chairs—chairs that I realized we would have to move ourselves. This made me very anxious. At Grace Cathedral, we would not provide a warm welcome to tourists who came in and moved our chairs. We had attempted to contact Chartres officials by letter and fax, but to no avail. It was clear that we were on our own. We had come all this way, and I had to experience the Chartres labyrinth firsthand. The labyrinth I had walked in the conference center at the Mystery School was a temporary one, taped onto the floor. It was not set up according to the specific proportions dictated by the system of sacred geometry. I needed to experience the ancient authenticity of the Chartres labyrinth. I counted the chairs. There were 256 of them. I didn't sleep much that night.

The next morning we met as planned. To bolster our courage, we decided to have coffee and pastries first. We went on to the cathedral and asked first at the gift shop if we could speak to a church official. Receiving no response, we decided to take things into our own hands. Two members of our group did not get involved in moving the chairs, in case we got into trouble and needed their help. The other four of us moved all the chairs without anyone asking any questions. Once the labyrinth was cleared, we held hands and said a brief prayer. I had the honor of entering the labyrinth first. My five friends and colleagues followed. About twenty-five tourists were in the cathedral at the time. They all walked the labyrinth as well. We were all left undisturbed for about an hour. Only when we began to put the chairs back were we confronted by a cathedral official.

I was thrilled to have had the chance to walk the labyrinth in Chartres Cathedral. It was truly powerful and drew me into a meditative state despite my uneasiness about walking it without permission. Everyone in our group felt an awesome, mysterious sense of grounding and empowerment from the walk. However, what attracted my attention most was that the cathedral seemed to come alive with excitement during our walk. The mood became light, fluid, and joyful in the dark and quiet space.

Looking back on that experience, I feel we had touched the Holy Spirit. Each of us had ventured to the center of our beings in the Chartres labyrinth that day. I received the embrace of Mary. I had, unknown to me at that time, ventured into her glorious web.

After our visit to Chartres, Barbara and I crossed the English Channel by boat and traveled to Magdalen College in Oxford. We had an appointment with Keith Critchlow for a brief breakfast meeting. When Dr. Critchlow greeted us, he was warm and welcoming. We immediately launched into the topic of the labyrinth. What did he mean by his references to "six psychological crises of humankind" and "sacred geometry"? There was so much to discuss, but there was one particular question I was burning to ask him: Did he think the labyrinth could be used as a spiritual tool? He confirmed my hopes and helped me clear the last hurdle in my mind. What seemed like a far-fetched idea was coming into clear focus. But this was the only answer we got. Our other questions were left unanswered as Dr. Critchlow rushed off to his class.

At that point we had only a name and a lot of ideas. The canvas labyrinth that would initially be used in Grace Cathedral had not yet been designed. But the experience of walking the labyrinth at Chartres and our meeting with Dr. Critchlow made it clear that there was nothing left to do but begin. I had myself confirmed beyond a doubt that this was a profound and powerful tool.

Seeking a Sacred Path

All of the larger-than-life questions about our presence here on earth and what gifts we have to offer are spiritual questions. To seek answers to these questions is to seek a sacred path. As we find our meaning and purpose we also realize that some invisible form of guidance has been leading us. We may not be able to recognize this in the moment, but in looking back over our lives we see the footprints of an invisible being that has guided us, challenged us, and carried us through times of crisis.

As seekers we may also feel that we missed our opportunity; that we may have chosen against this invisible life force. We may have been too afraid, or too tired to read the events in our lives, too attached to material things to give them up at the right time to start a new life. To live a life of regret is painful and difficult. Here lies the great gift of the Spirit: though we may have lost our way, when we come to that realization, we discover the path once again.

The spiritual hunger that is present in the Western world is calling forth millions of people. They

are seeking answers through a variety of paths rang-
ing from fundamentalism to various New Age spiritualities. Religious institutions of all faiths are
baffled at how to respond. The branch of the Christian church that is not tightly bound to a liturgical
tradition and believes in the sole authority of Scripture seems to be the first group to respond to our
chaotic times through fundamentalism. As fear for
our individual as well as collective future increases,
the flight into a literal interpretation of the Bible is
experiencing a dramatic revival. This fear breeds
small-mindedness and mean-spiritedness. The tyranny of the letter of the law, reflected in the Religious Right, is overshadowing the spirit of love that
was intended by the law of the Divine. The punishment of people who do not follow the rules is
becoming more predominant. And the rules are
becoming stricter and more difficult to obey
for the communities that do not have a represen-
tative voice. The shadow of the human spirit
that led to Hitler and World War II stalks us once
again.

Other religious institutions that have embraced
an open-minded stance to the dilemmas of being
human do not know how to respond. Institutions
with strong liturgical traditions are in the most challenging position. The open-minded Christian
church, with which I identify, unknowingly abandoned its teachings on how to nourish and nurture
the soul. The soul—that deep, hidden, knowing sense within—is malnourished. We mistakenly
thought that the intellect was the avenue to experiencing the Sacred, to nourishing the soul. We dis-

counted the imagination and our other faculties of knowing mystery.

Trust in the intellect began as an effort to keep in step with the trend toward rationalism developing over the last three centuries. The attack on blind faith went to the core of the churches' fears. Superstition, magic, and the distortions of faith that led to the slaughter of millions of people throughout history have impeded action on behalf of the Divine today. Most of us are aware of the severe limitations that rationalism has imposed upon the human spirit and the discovery of the Sacred. This has left churches needing to rethink their approach, their language, and the distance and boredom that rote liturgy can propagate. Church leaders are in the position of having to improvise programs rather than work from a script. Addressing the spiritual hunger of our age is not an easy task. And though the church may be aware of its menacing presence, it frequently scoffs at the spiritual revolution that is taking place in the Western world.

There are so many forms of new spiritualities emerging that they are hard to talk about in one book. In my thinking, new spiritual approaches are divided into two groups. The first group stands in a tradition, most frequently from the East, and has adapted its teachings to the Western mind. This may include Buddhist, Sufi, and Hindu teachings that have been transplanted here and have all determined themselves closer or farther from the tradition of their homeland. The second group of spiritualities comes from a potpourri of teachings— from the world of psychotherapy and holistic health, the recovery movement, and the creative arts or from the experiences of the extended consciousness that has become the experimental ground for many seekers. This would include seekers who are reading channeled material for guidance, experimenting with automatic writing, out-of-body experiences, and transcendental meditation to name only a few approaches.

There are dangers inherent in seeking a spiritual life. For those of us who abandon our critical thinking faculty to dependence on a charismatic leader, the trap of being caught in a cult is a real concern. For those hungry seekers who do not find a tradition, the discovery of disjointed teachings is like eating junk food. In the long run, the nourishment to sustain us is not there. The church doesn't understand many of the factors that are fueling the spiritual revolution, so its leaders tend to focus on these dangers. They fail to realize that people everywhere are looking for guidance. The church needs to forge a new identity, one that provides spiritual guidance and nurtures creativity.

"You need chaos in your soul to give birth to a dancing star," said Nietzsche. People need to awaken, to come to through the haze of physical existence and get a glimpse of the mystery behind life. The many spiritualities help to provide a pathway for people seeking what they think the church no longer provides—a connection to the Sacred within the context of a cosmos that holds the dancing stars. One woman saw the labyrinth as her connection and wrote to me saying:

As soon as I started to read the New York Times article my entire being resonated. It was as if the labyrinth were a magnet and my heart were a piece of metal. A voice inside of me cried, "Yes, yes, yes . . ." "I want to walk this." "I want to make one of them." "I want to bring this into the world." I see the labyrinth as an incredible gift. It is grace busting into our experience to help us be the co-creators we are instead of the "creation-destroyers" we have become. It is precisely because I do not understand "how it works" that I trust and honor it. Our thinking that we understand so much and are running the show is our downfall. I see the labyrinth as proof that at one time human beings were in touch with the right side of their brain. They were able to honor things that could not be explained by reason. Their worship was not simply from the neck up. I hear the Communion of Saints—our brothers and sisters who built Chartres—calling out to us. They see the desperate mess we are in and they are trying to help us to be who we really are. They are sharing with us one of their tools. Perhaps the only result of walking the labyrinth may be to notice that there exists another part of you that is speaking to you—no small result! This is the part we must nourish, honor, and listen to if we are to help save our world.

For me to walk the labyrinth would be an act of praise and thanksgiving. A moving Gloria to this other part of me that has been reborn; an act of surrender to the only God that I am able to trust.

The labyrinth, in its strange and uncanny way, offers a sacred and stable space to focus the attention and listen to the longing of the soul.

The Great-grandmother's Thread

As I searched for a way to describe what walking the labyrinth can mean, literally and metaphorically, I remembered George Macdonald's fairy tale *The Princess and the Goblin*. A young princess is sent away from her father's kingdom, away from the world, to a castle of supposed safety. She begins to explore her new home and encounters an old woman spinning thread in the tower. The woman introduces herself as the princess's great-grandmother. She tells the princess that she has awaited her for years. In time, the great-grandmother gives the princess a ring to which she attaches an invisible thread. This thread, the great-grandmother tells the princess, will guide her through the challenges she meets in life. The child is disappointed in her gift because she cannot see the thread or the ball that it comes from, which remains with the great-grandmother.

This fairy tale captures a glimpse of what it is like to walk a sacred path. By following an invisible thread we connect to the Source, to the Sacred. We can't see it, and yet some deep part of us knows it is there. This innate awareness gives us solace and peace during stormy times. But it is difficult to find at first, even difficult to believe.

To walk a sacred path is to know and trust that there is guidance to help us live our lives on this planet. Guidance can come in many, many ways. It comes through synchronistic meetings, through being fully present in one moment of time, through informal ritual where one spoken word can break open a riddle that has stumped us for months. Guidance also comes through forms, patterns, and symbols that impart sacred meaning. "That is precisely the great dignity of the symbol, that it . . . leads from the truths of the physical life to those of a higher spiritual order." Not only are we welcome to participate in these patterns or processes, our life does not take on ultimate meaning until we do. To discover the thread is to realize that a loving presence or force behind all the world urges us to risk our comfort and reach for meaning in our lives.

The great-grandmother's thread is the God within who has long been ignored and forgotten, who awaits discovery in our own castles. It is easy to forget something that is invisible, and yet that is the spiritual challenge. We must keep alive the innate part of ourselves that holds on to the invisible thread. Historically many forces have destroyed the memory of the great-grandmother's thread. It has been destroyed through centuries of patriarchal domination, through fears of creativity and of the traits associated with the feminine, such as empathy, curiosity, community, and holistic thinking. Mistrust of the imagination has been engendered through centuries of power politics that have little to do with nurturing the Spirit within.

The challenge of discovery looms large because the thread is invisible. Educated in scientific humanism at the end of the twentieth century, we are casualties of our history in both the personal and the collective sense. The traditional God is a God "out there," a transcendent God who acts through history—a God outside of ourselves who keeps track of whether we follow the rules. This transcendent God is more associated with God the Father, who no longer satisfies the deep hunger in our souls.

In the fairy tale, the source of the thread is hidden, but attached to the princess's ring. To walk a sacred path, each of us must find our own touchstone that puts us in contact with the invisible thread. This touchstone can be nature (as it was for me early on), sharing with our friends, playing with our children, painting on our day off, or walking in the country. It may be the Sunday-morning liturgy and Eucharist. Walking a sacred path means that we know the importance of returning to the touchstone that moves us. The labyrinth can serve as a touchstone.

The labyrinth stands with a tradition that recaptures the feminine sense of the Source. It utilizes the imagination and the pattern-discerning part of our nature. It invites relationship and offers a whole way of seeing. When we allow ourselves to be whole, we allow new visions to emerge within us and within our cultures. Due to the loss of the feminine, many of us are out of touch with the depths of our beings, our Source. The feminine must be enlivened and welcomed back into our male-dominated world so integration can begin to occur—between feminine and masculine, receptive and assertive, imagination and reason. But we are beginning to awaken, we are being freed to seek, we are feeling the restless force of our own longing. We long for healing and peace with the past. We long to know ourselves deeply, to know the place in which we can discover the Divine. We long to temper and hone our gifts, to put them in action in the world. Our times hold within them great challenges and great potential.

To walk a sacred path is to discover our inner sacred space: that core of feeling that is waiting to have life breathed back into it through symbols, archetypal forms like the labyrinth, rituals, stories and myths. Understanding the invisible world, the world of patterns and process, opens us up to the movement of the Spirit. Hildegard of Bingen was a twelfth-century mystic, composer, and author of a theology that knitted together nature and spirit, cosmos and soul. She described the Holy Spirit as the Greening Power of God. Just as plants are greened, so we are as well. As we grow up, our spark of life continually shines forth. If we ignore this spark, this greening power, we become thirsty and shriveled. And if we respond to the spark, we flower. Our task is to flower, to come into full blossom before our time comes to an end.

Blossoming, coming to full flower, gives quite a different sense of the Holy than we get in most churches today. "Religion is for those who are scared to death of hell. Spirituality is for those who have been there." A division has emerged in Western culture. We have confused religion with spirituality, the container with the process. Religion is the outward form, the "container," specifically the liturgy and all the acts of worship that teach, praise, and give thanks to God. Spirituality is the inward activity of growth and maturation that happens in each of us.

Spiritual growth can happen anywhere, anytime

when we are living consciously, reflecting on our experience. When our senses are shut down, when we live on automatic pilot, we miss the opportunity to grow. Age is not a measure of spiritual maturity. A young child with cancer can develop spiritually much faster than an adult who has never had such a confrontation, an awakening jolt. To be spiritually mature is to grow in an ever-deepening sense of compassion, lessening our fear of change and of the differences between us. Spiritual maturity also means knowing the vicissitudes of our personality as it experiences the Light of the Divine.

The challenge the church faces is to offer spiritual nurturance within, as well as outside, the religious service. Many seekers stay in a traditional worship setting briefly but leave the church with disappointment, feeling the lack of spiritual nourishment. The church is unable to help them with the transformations of their own lives. Spiritual seekers feel stultified by what seems to be a static and dogmatic tradition. This is what the church gives them week after week, instead of the treasures held within its mystical teachings. The beautiful flow and repeatable structure of church liturgy is designed for them to return to again and again. It is meant to nourish the soul. But it is not meeting the spiritual needs of our times.

Karen Armstrong, author of *The History of God*, tells of her struggle as a nun to find God when she had no direct personal experience:

> I *wish I would have learned this thirty years ago,*
> *when I was starting out in the religious life. It*
> *would have saved me a great deal of anxiety to*

*hear—from eminent monotheists in all three
faiths—that instead of waiting for God to descend
from on high, I should deliberately create a sense
of God for myself. Other rabbis, priests, and Sufis
would have taken me to task for assuming that
God was—in any sense—a reality "out there";
they would have warned me not to expect to experience God as an objective fact that could be discovered by the ordinary process of rational thought.
They would have told me that in an important
sense God was a product of the creative imagination, like the poetry and music that I found so inspiring.*

The product of the creative imagination, found
inside ourselves, not "out there" or above us—this is
what people are discovering in the labyrinth. It is a
container for the creative imagination to align with
our heart's desire, it is a place where we can pro-
foundly, yet playfully, experience our soul's longing
and intention.

Over the ages in the monastic traditions a discussion has continued as to whether people need a
direct experience of the numinous, Jung's word for
an experience with the Sacred, in order to serve
God. It is generally thought that we do not need a
direct experience of the Holy Spirit to sustain us.
An active prayer life and the fruits it produces are
thought to be enough to sustain people. Ruth Bur-
roughs, a Carmelite nun, in her book *Guidelines to
Mystical Prayer* makes a distinction between "lights-
on" and "lights-off" mysticism. Lights-on mysticism is explicit, conscious experiences of Divine

presence. These experiences awaken us, encourage us, and sustain us when our daily lives seems dry and uneventful. They help us discover that we are loved. Lights-off mysticism is devoid of direct, conscious contact with the Divine. Instead we are sustained through faith, the teachings of the church, and Scripture. I find this a helpful distinction. Karen Armstrong had a lights-off experience that was not enough to sustain her over a long period of time. Her experience resonates with many of us today. Our need is too great, and the reward too subtle, to settle for what seems like going through the motions without even a glimpse of the presence of the mystery of God.

I have watched members of the clergy and seekers in the church over the years. And I have come to the conclusion that if we choose a spiritual path not enclosed in a monastic setting, we'd better have some personal experience of the Sacred. Otherwise we are like a therapist who has never had therapy. If we have never had the experience, how can we help others understand what they are living through? Or we're like a painter who has never painted a picture. We have an image somewhere inside us, but neither we nor the world will ever benefit from it.

Lights-On Experiences

When I arrived home from my trip to Chartres, it was late August 1991. I decided to begin making a labyrinth for Grace Cathedral. I priced bolts of fabric and decided that 10-gauge canvas would be the most viable way to go. With the help of many volunteers, we sewed six heavy canvas panels together. The seven-by-forty-two-foot strips were attached with Velcro so that the labyrinth would be portable. We painstakingly painted the ancient pattern in purple onto the canvas, then cut it into an octagonal shape.

I was scheduled to do a presentation at the Common Boundary Conference on Sacred Stories that November, in Washington, D.C. Somehow, we finished the labyrinth in time. This was the first time the canvas from Grace Cathedral was offered to the public. We had no idea how it would be received. But for many of those first one hundred and forty people who walked it, time seemed to stand still. What some thought was five minutes turned out to be sixty. Some felt it immediately as a metaphor for their spiritual lives.

One woman in her early seventies walked into the labyrinth, meditated in the center, then unconsciously walked in a straight line out to its edge. She thought she had completed the walk. Then, watching others, she realized that she had not really completed the path. She asked to go in again, and this time she completed the walk on the path winding back out from the center. Later she told me that she had struggled all her life with completion issues. Until her moments on the labyrinth she had never seen how pervasive they were. She tearfully acknowledged to me, and to herself, just how much unfinished business she had in her life—how it troubled her more with every passing year.

Another person reported, "I loved the labyrinth!

This is the finest metaphor for my spiritual life I have ever experienced. It is truly sacred space." Opening the labyrinth to the public was like opening the floodgates of a dam—there was no way of containing it; there was no going back. Things would never be the same again.

We opened the labyrinth in Grace Cathedral on December 30, 1991, at six p.m. for twenty-four hours during a year's-end event called Singing for Your Life. A single newspaper article was enough to alert the public that something very special was happening at the cathedral. The waiting line for the labyrinth lasted from six p.m. until midnight. Despite my efforts to encourage people to sit down, or go downstairs for refreshments until the rush passed, they insisted on staying in line to watch as they waited. Watching other people walk can be a powerful meditation in its own right. From March 1992 until April 1994 we have had the canvas labyrinth open twice a month in the nave of the cathedral. The Tuesday after Easter in 1994 we dedicated a new labyrinth floor tapestry—a one-piece wool carpet, thirty-six feet in diameter. The installation of the labyrinth floor tapestry has allowed the labyrinth to be available daily for anyone who walks into Grace Cathedral. In June 1995 a permanent outdoor labyrinth made from terrazzo stone was laid in the Interfaith Garden, outdoors in the new cathedral close. This third labyrinth is forty feet in diameter and will be open to the public twenty-four hours a day.

Why does the labyrinth attract people? Because it is a tool to guide healing, deepen self-knowledge, and empower creativity. Walking the labyrinth clears the mind and gives insight into the spiritual journey. It urges action. It calms people in the throes of life transitions. It helps them see their lives in the context of a path, a pilgrimage. They realize that they are not human beings on a spiritual path but spiritual beings on a human path. To those of us who feel we have untapped gifts to offer, it stirs the creative fires within. To others who are in deep sorrow, the walk gives solace and peace. The experience is different for everyone because each of us brings different raw material to the labyrinth. We bring our unique hopes, dreams, history, and longings of the soul.

One woman who felt deeply alienated as the result of incest and abuse in her family came to walk the labyrinth. Fearing that the walk alone would intensify her feelings of isolation, she asked a friend to walk with her. As they made their way to the center together, the woman wept. She was experiencing many of the fears from her past. But she was able to walk through them, continuing her long journey of healing.

At the same walk was a man who was adopted but had no information about his family of origin. During his walk, he began to realize how much he needed to connect with his family to solidify his sense of self. He was surprised at these thoughts, as they emerged from his subconscious. He made a decision while on the labyrinth to begin the search for his birth parents. When he arrived home from the conference, there was a message on his answering machine from his birth mother. With wondrous synchronicity, the labyrinth walk had prepared him for meeting his other family. Later, when I was with the labyrinth at the Washington National Cathedral, I heard from a mutual friend that the man had attended a reunion where he met eighty relatives.

A woman at a drama therapists' conference in San Francisco came out of the labyrinth and gave me an unself-conscious hug. That morning she had awakened to a voice in her mind saying "I love . . . I love . . ." She could not figure it out, and after she played with it—"I love my husband, I love my son"—she put it aside. On the labyrinth she heard the same voice saying "I love *you*," and she was overcome with joy, realizing how deeply she is loved by God.

That connection with Spirit is possible within the wondrous container of the labyrinth. As thoughts dispel, we invite into our awareness an open-minded attention. This consciousness moves out of focus the events in our lives and allows us to see that it is the invisible moments between the events that are important. Robert Lawlor uses a Buddhist analogy to capture this: "Time is like a necklace of square beads of tangible objects, or moments or events, and to be absorbed by this succession of limited frames is maya or illusion, whereas only the inner thread of the necklace, the unimaginable continuum, is reality." The labyrinth awaits our discovery, for it will guide us through the troubles of our lives to the grand mysterious patterns that shape the web of creation. It will lead us toward the Source and eventually guide us home.

NEW PILGRIMS,
NEW PATHS

There are two approaches to the Divine, both spiral. One is an inward process of regeneration and integration, achieved with the aid of a mandala, and is a concentration into and through the centre; the other is the outward pilgrimage of Parsifal, Gilgamesh or Jason. The essential unity of the two is illustrated by the inward spiral of Bunyan's Pilgrim's Progress to the Celestial City, of Dante's climb to the summit of Mount Purgatory, and of Sudama's journey to the Golden City of Krishna.

—Jill Purce, The Mystic Spiral

All the great world religions contain teachings that articulate the journey of the spiritual seeker; the path one must walk in order to grow in compassion and respond to the world with clarity and wisdom. In essence, the task is to grow the "substance of the soul." In Buddhist teachings this is called the path to Enlightenment. In the Hindu tradition moksha (freedom) is sought. And in Christianity, union with God through self-knowledge is the end point.

Some paths draw us into ourselves; others usher us out into the world to explore, to learn, and to serve. Characteristically, the West has emphasized action in the world with little recognition of contemplation. The East has done the opposite, placing greater value on meditative spirituality. But as Eastern teachings become transplanted in Western soil, we are beginning to appreciate the worth of turning inward. Ram Dass, the Hindu spiritual teacher, talks about meditation as the search for a spaciousness within. Both Eastern and Western traditions can guide us to this place where our soul resides and guides us as we journey through life. The integration of contemplative and active approaches is strengthening the spiritual revolution that has begun in the West.

We each need to take stock of ourselves. We need to be shaken out of our complacency and begin to use our short time here creatively so we don't look back in regret. And if we come up missing, our hope lies in finding the strength to change. To be pilgrims walking on a path to the next century, we need to participate in the dance between silence and image, ear and eye, inner and outer. We need to change our seeking into discovery, our drifting into pilgrimage. In the Christian tradition there are two ways of approaching the path to the Sacred, the Apopathic path and the Kathopathic path.

The Path through Silence

The path through silence is called the Apopathic path. It is the path of meditation or contemplation which leads us to the center of our being. We plant the seed of silence within ourselves by quieting the mind. We allow our minds to empty of thought so we can enter our own resounding silence, a state from which we gain deep refreshment. Gregory the Great called this state "resting in God." Experiencing the silence within is like opening a hidden door to the soul. It takes enormous patience. Thomas Keating, a Cistercian monk who teaches this method of contemplation, calls it centering prayer.

The path of silence demands a disciplined concentration that many of us do not have the ability to sustain amid the chaos of our stressful lives. However, the amount of stress that we are under is what makes it so crucial that we find a method of meditation. If we do not develop this outlet in our lives, we have no way to reach the spaciousness within that allows us to move with the flow of our complex world. The labyrinth can be a tremendous help in quieting the mind, because the body is moving. Movement takes away the excess charge of psychic energy that disturbs our efforts to quiet our thought processes.

The Path through Images

The Kathopathic path uses the imaginative process as a guide to the Light within. However, the path through images has traditionally been less honored than the path through silence. It is enjoying a revitalization partly because of various therapeutic approaches bolstering research in this area so that we know more about how images are formed. Guided visualization, one form of encouraging images, has gained public acceptance as well.

The first step on the Kathopathic path is also to quiet the mind. We need to reach a level of consciousness where we are not flooded with extraneous thought. We want to be open to our experience, to enter a receptive state that allows images to appear. Images may seem like self-conscious actors being pushed out from behind the curtains on our inner stage, until they get used to being invited to communicate with us. These images then may remain singular and silent before us or they may unfold within our soul's eye. The imagination guides the thoughts that occur in relation to the image, rather than the imagination being guided by the thought process as in everyday consciousness.

One woman walked into the center of the labyrinth and saw a large red beating heart. She had no knowledge of the sacred heart tradition in Christianity and was simply awed and puzzled by what she saw. The images that come from the unconscious mind, especially when we are in a sacred setting, can be gifts of Divine grace. It takes work to unearth and decipher these messages from the collective unconscious.

In Kathopathic prayer the meditator never really abandons the mental process. It becomes like a paddle that guides the canoe of the heart through the waters flowing to the soul. The mind, when quieted and expanded beyond everyday consciousness, opens a path to the sacred through the gift of the imagination. Images offered up through our creative imaginations can help us heal our broken psyches, and discover new capacities. We feel joy because we know the sacred act of healing is taking place. It is then we know the connection with the Spirit, the pull of the great-grandmother's thread.

Historically, the path through silence has been thought superior to the path through images. Many think the Kathopathic path is less reliable because it involves the imagination. Unfortunately this attitude is based on an early translation of the word *imagination*. The Greek word for the imagination is *fantasia*, which translates as "fantasy." Fantasy and imagination came to be seen as one and the same thing. "The imagination," writes Alan Ecclestone, "brings the whole soul into activity, unlike fantasy which is one-dimensional: it plays with things without paying anything for them. Fantasy is not costly whereas the imagination is strenuous. Holding things together is hard work."

I think of the path through silence and the path through images as two great rivers that converge. Those who have closely observed the dance of silence and image agree that when one is resting in the heart of silence an image appears. And when one receives a profound image, a great silence envelops the soul. Both paths require a new and different level of consciousness. Both paths invite another level of consciousness by diminishing distracting thoughts. Both paths may be discovered in the labyrinth. One seeker wrote:

> My journey in the labyrinth yielded far more than I had expected. I experienced the walk itself as such a wonderful metaphor for the way I walk my days: just as it was meant to be. Trusting/not trusting in the path, my ability to follow it, whether it was the "right" one, sitting in the center and listening to the word "open" pulse through me. Although the words of the messages (or the silence) we receive vary greatly, at root I believe all the wisdom leads us to one place: healing, connection and love for all of life.

The Inner Way: The Threefold Mystical Plan

In Western Christianity the mystical path is traditionally called the Threefold Path. The three stages that define the sequence, the process we experience as an ever-deepening sense of union with the Divine, are Purgation, Illumination, and Union. The hope is for self-knowledge and knowledge of one's relationship to the Divine. This is the path that is energetically embedded in the labyrinth design.

"Mysticism—in a very broad definition—is the experience of communion with Ultimate Reality." In Christian mystical tradition, knowledge of self and knowledge of God are one. If you have gone deeply within yourself and experienced mystery of your being, the mystery of God reveals itself. Knowing the depths of our being, both the shadow and the light, introduces us to the vastness of the Spirit, the Sacred held within each of us.

Purgation, the walk from the entrance of the labyrinth to its center, represents the first part of the mystical path. *Purgation* is an archaic word, from the root "to purge"—to release, to empty, to quiet. I often experience it as shedding. We let go of the things that block communication with our Higher Power. We relinquish the things that we attempt to control. It is believed that the monks and pilgrims walked the first part of the labyrinth on their knees as a penitential act, to humble themselves before God. In order to come before the Holy One, whether we envision this force inside or outside ourselves, we need to surrender our daily concerns.

Illumination, the second stage of the Threefold Path, may be found in the center of the labyrinth. Usually it is a surprise to reach the center because the long winding path seems so "illogical." We don't know we're there until we're there, which is often true in life. Being fully present in the moment is the key to realizing the potential of time. After we have quieted the mind on the labyrinth's path, the center is a place for meditation and prayer. Here people find insight into their problems; their lives are illuminated. We may come to clarity in the center. If we enter with an open heart and mind, we will be able to receive what is there for us.

Union begins as we leave the center of the labyrinth, following the same path back out that brought us in. In this stage, our meditation often produces a grounded, empowered feeling. Many people who have had an important experience in the center feel that this third stage of the walk gives them a way of integrating the insight they have gained. Others feel that it stokes the creative fires within. It energizes the insight. It invites us, empowers us, even pushes us to be more authentic. It gives us the confidence to take risks as we manifest our gifts in the world.

Union means communing, or communion with the Holy. In the mystical tradition of the Middle Ages, it meant being completely absorbed by God. The monastic orders based their life together on a fulfilling balance between their work and the many hours of worship in their daily lives. Our times present a similar challenge. We are struggling to find a balance between our work, sleep, family and friends, leisure and attention to our spiritual lives. The lack of structured communities that share work responsibilities and the highly individualistic nature of our society make the task of finding balance even more difficult.

The monastic communities offered a mystical spirituality that spoke to highly intuitive and intensely introverted people, and at the same time provided economic structure throughout Europe.

Monasteries provided schools and hospitals managed by monks, yet their cloistered life helped them stay inwardly directed. Today, without any reliable structure directing us, the way of union needs to be rethought. Our times call for most of us to be outer-directed. The majority of people involved in spiritual transformation are searching for a path that guides them to serve the world in an active, self-aware, compassionate way. The third stage of the labyrinth walk empowers the seeker to move back out into the world, replenished and directed. This is what makes the labyrinth a particularly powerful tool for transformation. It helps mend the split between contemplation and action that has hindered spiritual work in the world.

One pilgrim described her path in a letter:

> It is amazing to me that the "same" labyrinth—the "same" spiritual journey for each of us—generates an incredible variety of experience and insights for each individual, just as we each walked "our" path in a unique way. I was also very much aware (for the first time) that the path of purgation and the path of union are the same path! This still fascinates and draws me, and I haven't fully come to understand what it means—rich fodder for meditations to come.

The Outer Way: Pilgrimage

The tradition of pilgrimage is as old as religion itself. Worshipers traveled to holy festivals: to solstice celebrations, to circumambulations around the Ka'aba in Mecca for the high holy days of Islam, or to Easter festivals in Jerusalem. Pilgrimages were a mixture of religious duty and holiday relaxation for the commoner and the rich landowner alike. The journey was often done in groups with designated areas along the route for shelter at night. Pilgrims were restless to explore mystical holy places like Chartres, Lourdes, and Mont Saint Michel. Many were in search of physical or spiritual healing. In the Middle Ages, most people did not read and were much more oriented to the senses than we are today. The Christian story, which emphasized the humanity of Christ, held great fascination for the pilgrims. Many learned it by going to Jerusalem to walk where Jesus walked, to pray where he prayed, and to experience a solemn moment where he died.

Usually early in life, Christians in the Middle Ages made a vow: to make a pilgrimage to the Holy City of Jerusalem once during their life. However, by the twelfth century, when the Crusades swept across Europe and Jerusalem became the center of religious struggle, travel became dangerous and expensive. In response to this situation, the Roman church appointed seven pilgrimage cathedrals to become the "Jerusalem" for pilgrims. The walk into the labyrinth in many of these cathedrals marked the ritual ending of the physical journey across the countryside. It served as a symbolic entry into the spiritual realms of the Celestial City.

Images of the Celestial City of Jerusalem from the book of Revelation to John were reflected in the wondrous Gothic cathedrals of the Middle Ages.

The walls of the cathedrals were painted in bright colors, so when they were illuminated by the sun, the stained-glass windows created a mosaic of colorful, dancing jewels. This holy atmosphere of beauty reverberated in the religious imagination of the pilgrims as they encountered the awesome mystery of the City of God. In the tradition of pilgrimage, the path of the labyrinth is called the Chemin de Jerusalem—the road to Jerusalem—and the center of the labyrinth, the New Jerusalem.

The tradition of pilgrimage is being revitalized during our own times to seek answers to our longings. "Pilgrims are person in motion," writes Richard R. Niebuhr, "passing through territories not their own—seeking something we might call completion, or perhaps the word *clarity* will do as well, a goal to which only the spirit's compass points the way." The pilgrim seeks to follow the spirit's compass which guides us to find an inner openness to the outer world of people, places, and events that become the fabric of our lives.

Rediscovering
the Act of Pilgrimage

In June 1992, I attended the International Transpersonal Association conference in Prague. The program was called Science, Spirituality and the Global Crisis. One of the speakers, English biologist Rupert Sheldrake, was asked where he would begin to effect change in the world. How could people begin to grapple with the global crisis? He said, "I would change tourism into pilgrimage, help tourists become pilgrims." Chills went up my spine.

At Grace Cathedral, we had been working with the theme of pilgrimage for three years through Quest. Our setting seemed perfect. The trustees, dean, and chapter on which I serve are custodians of a grand and beautiful sacred space. It is located in the center of one of the most welcoming and intriguing cities in the world. Our canvas labyrinth had been available to the public for six months by then. Each time it was open, at least one hundred and fifty people from various spiritual paths turned up to walk it. It had captured the imagination of believers and nonbelievers alike. I realized the labyrinth was not just a symbol for pilgrimage—we were providing sacred space for anyone seeking transformation. We were providing a destination for modern pilgrims.

What is the difference between a pilgrim and a tourist? I sat in a church in Prague contemplating this question. Watching people enter the church, I observed that tourists take pictures. Pilgrims may also, but they go farther: they sit and meditate, some kneel in prayer, some light candles.

I thought about my trip to Chartres the previous summer. After our group went its separate ways, Barbara and I spent many hours in the cathedral. After we measured the labyrinth we sat by the veil of Mary, the relic that had helped make Chartres famous during the Middle Ages and was said to hold great healing powers. It was a moving experience to sit prayerfully in the chapel, surrounded by others in a state of deep devotion. We lit candles for our families, our friends, and for Grace Cathedral, that it may be a beacon of light to all who travel there. I lit a candle for the Labyrinth Project. When traveling as pilgrims we come with vulnerability and humility. We fear that we may be unwelcome. When we moved the chairs in Chartres Cathedral, we crossed the line between observation and participation. The pilgrim participates. The tourist observes.

Rediscovering this magnificent spiritual tool is an idea whose time has come. It is both a challenge and an honor to place the labyrinth back into sacred space—to share it with the countless numbers of people who seek a spiritual mooring. Now I sit writing a book about the labyrinth. I travel around the country with the labyrinth and continue the Labyrinth Project at Grace Cathedral. I try to meet numerous requests for workshops and information on making labyrinths. The shift from tourist, who comes with an interested eye, to pilgrim, who comes with a searching heart, makes all the difference in the world.

Healing

What are modern-day pilgrims searching for? Through my years of work as a psychotherapist in New York City and as a priest at Grace Cathedral, I have realized that spiritual hunger has three major facets: We need healing. We long to be co-creators with Divine forces. We seek self-knowledge.

Psychological healing is one of the most pressing issues of our time. Many of us carry psychological and spiritual burdens from our past that hinder us in the present. We may come from a difficult and unsupportive family situation. We may have lost a parent at a young age. We may be struggling out of a painful divorce. We may have been the victim of a crime, our trust in others shattered. Whatever our difficulty, we sense that we cannot live fully because of our wounds.

When we are carrying the burdens of the past, our relationships suffer and our creativity is limited. The labyrinth can provide a safe container for shedding these burdens. One Sunday, a woman came to walk the labyrinth. She was struggling with a number of the friendships in her life. When she entered the labyrinth and quieted her mind, she began to see the unity of the whole. She noticed that her place in relationship to others changed as she walked. She saw other walkers from the back and from the side. Some were flowing with a silent melody of their own. Some were joyful, some solemn. Some remained near her, others brushed by as they completed their walk. In the human rhythm of the walk, the woman was able to see that she had unrealistic expectations of her friends and family. She assumed they saw the world just as she did. And when they didn't, she felt betrayed and abandoned. She saw for the first time that everyone was on the same path, but at a different place in their own journey through life.

Each experience in the labyrinth is unique, and many are healing. Divisions we thought were "real" dissolve before our eyes. One young woman experienced the labyrinth during a Lenten Quiet Day. Though she was successful and enjoyed her career, she was alone in life. She felt it was "God's will" that she would never marry. She was walking the labyrinth to help reconcile her sense of loss. But in the labyrinth she heard a voice say, "I wouldn't ask that of you . . ." In that moment, she realized the idea that career and marriage were mutually exclusive was her own creation.

Many tears have been shed on the labyrinth. At a Women's Dream Quest workshop, one woman who came to walk the labyrinth said to me, "If I start crying, I will never stop." I encouraged her to let herself cry. I guessed that this was most likely why she came in the first place. She had experienced a double mastectomy and a divorce within a year's time. Her grief was deep, and her fear was all-encompassing. She cried long and hard. And afterward she was radiant.

Crying for yourself can heal deep wounds. This is not the same as feeling sorry for yourself, which happens when the ego is in control but feels helpless. Compunction comes from the heart. The heart cries for us as we recognize our wounds, our human limitations. A Sufi verse says, "When the heart weeps for what it's lost, the soul rejoices for what it's found." Compunction ends in gentleness and a renewed patience with ourselves—an acknowledgment that the path through life can be extremely difficult. Walking the labyrinth gives comfort to the aching heart, and solace to the weary soul. It can go beyond the bounds of comfort that another human being can give.

Forgiveness is frequently the bridge between psychological and spiritual healing. We can do the hard work of experiencing anger and admitting that we blame the people who have hurt us. But we must authentically give it all up, offer it to the Holy Spirit, before we can receive the gift that a hurtful experience has hidden within. Inner absolution sometimes occurs in the labyrinth. We may be freed from guilt and released to greet the future that celebrates the gift of life. The labyrinth can offer the sacred space where healing through forgiveness may occur. Modern pilgrims have walked into an unknown path and experienced resurrection.

Many people seek strength in the wake of physical illness. Groups of people with AIDS have come to the labyrinth to find courage to carry on their struggle. One man described his labyrinth experience as "being mentally lost and spiritually found." The mother of this man carried the heavy burden of her son's illness into the center of the labyrinth and surrendered it to God. Since that time, she has felt less isolated from her son. She is free to be close and loving in their relationship because she knows he is supported by a Higher Power. One congregation member walked the labyrinth every day for a month as he healed, physically and emotionally, from a gallbladder operation. A woman with cystic fibrosis came to a workshop in New Canaan, Connecticut, and found that she felt physically strengthened while walking the labyrinth. Healing on the labyrinth comes in the form of renewed strength and perspective that is needed when illness has made us vulnerable.

Co-Creation

We long to be co-creators with the powerful forces of Light that guide human existence. Much of our spiritual seeking is driven by the desire to manifest our unique and individual gifts in the world. Søren Kierkegaard said, "Every human being comes to earth with sealed orders." Many of us sense this. Something within us carries a deep, sometimes buried, sense that we have a special task. However, we need the tools to find our orders and decipher them. Many people find their way to the labyrinth in the process of searching for their own special talents. They come for insight into how their unique skills can serve the world. Spiritual restlessness is rampant because many of us feel that we are not using our gifts.

Our educational system rarely helps us find a place where we can make a true contribution to society. Choice of profession has become foremost a decision about providing financial security for our families. The American Dream is about security, not about the force of passion that can serve as the guiding principle for our lives. There are hundreds of thousands of us ill-suited to the work we are doing, searching unsuccessfully for passion in our work. We are longing to contribute creatively to our society, to help heal the planet.

This is not a job-training issue, it is a soul-level issue. Whether or not we stand within a religious tradition, there is a desire within each person to create and to contribute in a way that gives satisfaction. This is the longing of co-creation, the search for wholeness through service. This is the essence of spiritual transformation. Our work in the world can become a Holy Act. The labyrinth is a transformative tool that can help people discover their "sealed orders." The modern pilgrim seeks a passionate connection to his or her individual gifts, and the grace to use them to better humankind.

Self-Knowledge

In the Christian tradition there is an emphasis on the shadow—the dark side of humankind for which each person must take responsibility. Exploration of the shadow is one of the most important goals of Christian spirituality. Carl Jung defined the shadow as the collection of all the parts of our personality that were not accepted by the ego. The ego impedes our journey and encourages the shadow. It is the purpose of all spiritual disciplines, in all religious traditions, to move beyond the human ego. Do not misunderstand: the human ego is necessary. As Jung noted, the task of the first part of life is to build and strengthen the ego. We need the ego to manage our personalities. It is the part of us that makes the decisions. What am I going to wear today? Whom shall we invite to dinner next Friday? All the details of everyday life need attention. The more healthy our ego, the more efficiently we live our lives.

However, when it comes to spiritual matters the ego must downshift. Once the tasks of the first half of life (career, marriage, and family) are accomplished, the ego must learn to relinquish control. This may be perceived as a threat to the ego, especially when it serves as a guardian against recognizing anger and fear. A spiritual discipline is designed to release control of the ego so the "Light behind the mind" can come into focus. This is the silence of the ages that gives us rest. This is where we meet God.

When the ego begins to let go, we can meet the shadow part of ourselves. Getting to know our shadow is perhaps the most important spiritual work we can do at this time. The ego develops a certain identity and when thoughts, feelings, or behaviors contradict that identity, it may simply disown them. Often our only hint that we are fighting our shadow is a feeling of being stuck. We are not growing and maturing as we had hoped. The shadow is the scrap pile of rejected emotions that are stored beneath our conscious awareness. But the shadow creates an energy of its own, gaining more power the longer it is denied. The shadow tries to reveal itself in our thoughts, feelings, and behaviors, but the ego often prevents us from noticing. We remain insensitive to our impact on others and unconscious of the feelings fermenting within. However, in order to mature spiritually we must recognize our shadow emotions as our own. Having the labyrinth, a place to meet ourselves, to see and own our shadows, is a revolutionary step.

Does the pilgrim's journey ever end? Perhaps not as long as we traverse this earthly plane. As the physical body continues to age we become increasingly aware of life's transition, of life's progression.

But is there an end to the search? Yes, perhaps there is. For many of the thousands who have walked the labyrinth, there has to be a clearer understanding of a fascinating paradox. Although we do not have the thing that we seek, in order to sense its lack we must have some foreknowledge of it. We have a hidden sense of what we need, otherwise we would not be driven to the search. "Unless we also carry within our hearts the God whom we are seeking, we will never find God."

A Wide and Gracious Path

One of the Christian images that is reimagined in the labyrinth is the "straight and narrow" path. The labyrinth's path is narrow, but far from straight. The straight and narrow image implies that we can make mistakes or lose our way. The path of life is not easy, and we do make mistakes. But few, if any, are beyond the mercy of God. Losing our way in life is not only a possibility, it is an experience that is part of the spiritual path. We often don't realize that the way to God is generous and error is part of the journey. As soon as we become conscious that we are lost, we have found our way again. The path of the labyrinth is also forgiving. One person recounted her experience:

On the return out of the center, somehow I missed the path and returned a second time to the center. There I heard God's reassurance: "Go ahead. Sometimes you have to repeat the path, but you

will be held at the center." I let things flow after
that, and some amazing energy flowed. Healing
energy. I am deeply awed.

Another way of gauging your own inner assump-
tions about the straight and narrow path is to ask
yourself how wide you envision Jacob's ladder to be.
In my mind's eye, it was always wide enough for one
person. Then I saw William Blake's amazing painting *Jacob's Ladder*, in which the path from earth to
heaven is as wide as a four-lane highway. And it is
graciously curved and flowing, connecting heaven
and earth. People are strolling arm in arm, some
going up, some going down. It communicates a gen-
erosity about the Divine that we long to experience.

The labyrinth introduces us to the idea of a wide
and gracious path. It redefines the journey to God:
from a vertical perspective that goes from earth up
to heaven, to a horizontal perspective in which we
are all walking the path together. The vertical path
has gotten mired down in perfectionist associations,
whereas the horizontal path communicates that we
are all in this together.

THE LABYRINTH:
SACRED PATTERN,
SACRED PATH

*The labyrinth is a model of spiritual cosmology that
is quite unrecognizable to the modern mentality since
this understanding disappeared after the acceptance
of Descartes' world view and the split of
the mind/body/spirit.*

—Keith Critchlow

Earliest-Known Labyrinths

Labyrinths are divine imprints. They are universal patterns most likely created in the realm of
the collective unconscious, birthed through the
human psyche and passed down through the ages.
Labyrinths are mysterious because we do not know
the origin of their design, or exactly how they provide a space that allows clarity.

Labyrinths can be found in almost every religious tradition around the world. The Kabbala, or Tree of Life, found in the Jewish mystical tradition is an elongated labyrinth figure based on the number 11. The Hopi medicine wheel, based on the number 4, and the Man in the Maze are just two of the many Native American labyrinths. Tibetan sand paintings, though not walked, are mandalas, a kind of labyrinth created through a meditative state. They hold the experience of transformation within them as well.

Labyrinths have been known to the human race for over four thousand years. The oldest European form on record is the Cretan labyrinth, also called the classical seven-circuit labyrinth. It is believed that these designs evolved out of the spiral figure found in nature. Possibly the oldest surviving labyrinth is found in a rock carving at Luzzanas in Sardinia, and dates from 2500–2000 B.C.E. Cretan labyrinths were also imprinted on coins and traced into pottery and other artifacts in ancient civilizations. Researchers note that even though early civilizations were isolated from one another, only one archetypal design of the labyrinth emerged over thousands of years. Remains of a seven-circuit labyrinth can be found on Mount Knossos, on the isle of Crete.

The earliest surviving labyrinth designs on a ceramic vessel (c. 1300 B.C.E.) were found at Tell Rifa'at, Syria, and on an inscribed clay tablet (c. 1200 B.C.E.) found at Pylos, Peloponnisos, Greece. Researchers suggest that the giant labyrinthine structure built at Fayum in Egypt by King Amenemhet III around 1800 B.C.E. was the first labyrinth construction that could be walked through. Herodotus, born about 484 B.C.E., is the first person known to have used the term "labyrinth."

Labyrinths are made of many materials. Some have paths outlined in stone. Others are carved into stone. The early Roman-style labyrinths were usually made of mosaic tile. Turf labyrinths, found throughout England, Scandinavia, and Germany are made from mounds of earth covered with grass. Our tapestry labyrinth at Grace Cathedral is wool, and our original portable labyrinth is a heavy canvas.

As I began studying labyrinths, I noted contradictions in the literature. Jean Favier, whose research is exquisitely detailed, says that "the labyrinth has never really been used for any religious practices." Some historians stated it was purely for decorative purposes. Other sources, including a recent labyrinth display at Chartres Cathedral, attest to the fact that labyrinths were walked in medieval times. My research goal was to learn enough to understand how the labyrinth works in the human psyche. I also needed to be able to transpose its dimensions so the form and proportion remained intact for our labyrinth at Grace Cathedral.

As I plunged into all the materials I had gathered, two terms gave me pause: "lost knowledge" and "sacred geometry." It is not unusual on our spiritual paths to be asked to do things that seem beyond our grasp. This is the way I felt beginning to write about sacred geometry. I took Euclidean geometry in tenth grade and barely got a passing grade. The basic principles eluded me. I remembered vividly the frustration of trying to understand something that did not speak to me in any way.

Now the labyrinth had returned me to a geometry with a not small blessing—the word *sacred* was attached. This time I was motivated to understand. This chapter, which just scratches the surface of sacred geometry, simply points in the right direction. If we are able to make our own labyrinths, we can begin to bring them into the lives of our communities. They can bring about the personal and communal transformation that is essential for the ultimate preservation of life on this fragile earth.

Robert Lawlor's *Sacred Geometry, Philosophy and Practice,* the most helpful book I found, served as a primer for me. It is rich in spiritual insights that are woven throughout the book. Sacred geometry is based on ancient, sacred knowledge that was articulated in architectural forms. It is a lost art that developed a balanced and serene climate for the human psyche and soul. Through proportion, placement, and position of stone, wood, and mortar— using a complementary system of numbers, angles, and design—the mind can find rest, comfort, and harmony. This leaves the mind open to other levels of awareness. The Chinese approach to these principles is a variation of traditional Chinese cosmology called Feng-shui. It is also enjoying a revival in the Western world.

The Gothic cathedrals of Europe were all created according to methods of applied sacred geometry. Labyrinths were strategically located in geometric patterns that related to the whole of the cathedral. This geometry is now, for the most part, a lost body of knowledge. According to Lawlor, the theory of sacred geometry stems from the philosopher Plato and the actual measurements and equations were developed by Pythagoras. Pythagorean geometry was based on whole numbers and did not use a zero. Though zero came into use around the eighth century, it was rejected by Bernard of Clairvaux and the Cistercians because zero undermined the numerical system based on 1. One was the symbolic number for unity within the cosmos. When the use of zero was finally accepted, knowledge of the Pythagorean system was lost and the symbol and sense of unity forgotten.

Sacred geometry was once considered a divine art, and master builders and masons were held in high esteem. Robert Lawlor explains:

For the human spirit caught within a spinning universe in an ever confusing flow of events, circumstance and inner turmoil, to seek truth has always been to seek the invariable, whether it is called Ideas, Forms, Archetypes, Numbers or Gods. To enter a temple constructed wholly of invariable geometric proportions is to enter an abode of eternal truth.

Sacred geometry is the key to creating "an abode of eternal truth." The architects approached this lofty ideal by embracing the concept and experience of unity, something we know little about in this postmodern age.

The whole of creation was seen as a source for

this sacred art. The central concept of unity, symbolized by the circle, stands behind the choice of numbers, proportions, and pattern. In essence, unity creates by dividing itself, so the basic challenge was to demonstrate how "absolute unity can become multiplicity and diversity." Unity and the number 1 were seen as the same thing. One was singular and as unity it was all inclusive. By this reasoning, 2 could not simply be two ones placed side by side as it is today. Mirroring the natural pattern of cells multiplying, it is not through addition that unity creates diversity but through division. Through the forms of Gothic architecture—the use of circles, squares, and rectangles—sacred geometry attempts to recapture the "orderly movement from an infinite formlessness to an endless interconnected array of forms, and in recreating this mysterious passage from One to Two, it renders it symbolically visible."

The Difference Between a Labyrinth and a Maze

I have noticed when I mention the word *labyrinth* to people without showing them an image, most people think of a maze. The word *maze* is also frequently used interchangeably with the word *labyrinth,* creating further confusion. This is understandable since the labyrinth has not been in use for approximately three hundred and fifty years. When I give my thumbnail sketch at the labyrinth to prepare people for their walk, I carefully explain that a

A Maze

labyrinth is different from a maze. Labyrinths are unicursal. They have one well-defined path that leads us into the center and back out again. There are no tricks to it, no dead ends or cul-de-sacs, no intersecting paths.

Mazes, on the other hand, are multicursal. They offer a choice of paths, some with many entrances and exits. Dead ends and cul-de-sacs present riddles to be solved. Mazes challenge the choice-making part of ourselves. Often they are made from hedges or other materials that create alleyways to limit the walkers' sight. Our logic is challenged. Here's one walker's experience:

> *As a truth seeker and pilgrim for many years, it was amazing to be on a journey that immediately revealed itself to me as a metaphor for my life. I always enjoyed mazes, knowing there was ultimately*

*a way out but having to find it was a game I en-
joyed. As I got older, the game became less fun,
the mazes more twisted, the challenges more ex-
hausting: another metaphor for my life. The
labyrinth is safe, effective and inspiring. I woke up
this morning with a poem coming through.*

The unicursal path of the labyrinth is what differentiates it and sets it apart as a spiritual tool. The
labyrinth does not engage our thinking minds. It invites our intuitive, pattern-seeking, symbolic mind
to come forth. It presents us with only one, but profound, choice. To enter a labyrinth is to choose to
walk a spiritual path.

Church Labyrinths

Church labyrinths, also known as pavement
labyrinths, make up their own specific cate-
gory. They are unicursal and are laid on or into the
floor. The earliest Christian labyrinth is most likely
the one found in the fourth-century basilica of
Reparatus, Orleansville, in Algeria. The words
Sancta Eclesia at the center confirm its use as a
Christian treasure. This pavement labyrinth was designed in the classical Roman style and is one of
many examples left in the world. In the Roman
labyrinth design, the path goes methodically from
quadrant to quadrant. This differentiates it from the
medieval Christian labyrinth, whose path meanders
through all four quadrants, instead of proceeding

Roman Labyrinth

one by one. The medieval labyrinth is considered a breakthrough in design because it is less linear, and it creates the feeling of not knowing where the path goes next. An early manuscript (c. 860 A.D.) contains a prototype of this medieval design. A more formal drawing appears again in a tenth-century Montpelier manuscript.

The earliest labyrinth appearing on a wall is believed to be at St. Lucca Cathedral in Italy and dates from the ninth century. This labyrinth, approximately eighteen by eighteen inches, was designed for people to trace with their fingers before they entered the cathedral. This was understood to be a way of quieting the mind before entering sacred space.

There are two styles of the classical eleven-circuit labyrinth. The circular design of the Chartres labyrinth is from the tradition of the Knights Templar. Legend says that the design was part of King Solomon's temple and was carried to France by the Templars. This style of labyrinth is also associated

Maltese Labyrinth

with the freemasons, the guilds that provided the expertise and the labor for the building of the Gothic cathedrals throughout Europe. The second style is from the Maltese tradition and can be seen in Amiens Cathedral, northwest of Paris. The same unicursal path is shaped octagonally there. When viewed from above, a Maltese cross can be seen within the pattern. The labyrinth at Amiens was restored in 1894 and, unlike the one at Chartres, is open daily. The public is encouraged to come and walk. The verger of Amiens Cathedral has published a pamphlet and loves to share his knowledge of the labyrinth with tourists and pilgrims.

While there are no known records of anyone walking the labyrinth, it is possible that the labyrinth was a major force in creative people's lives. Although I know of no Christian writers or artists who directly refer to the labyrinth as a spiritual tool,

the fact that it was so often pictured leads me to believe one of two things: that it was used as a matter
of course in the fabric of daily living, or that it was
used as a sacred tool that no one was allowed to talk
about.

There are many indirect references to the
labyrinth. Hildegard of Bingen defined divinity as "a
circle, a wheel, a whole." In the *Divine Comedy*,
Dante uses both the metaphor and the image of the
labyrinth. The winding path through Purgatory is a
labyrinthine journey. If you lifted up the center of
the labyrinth by the six three-quarter circles or
petals in the center, the eleven circles would fall or
wind downward in the exact image of Mount Purgation. When Dante arrives at the last circle of Par-
adise he is greeted by Beatrice, who hands him a
rose, a symbol associated with the center of the
labyrinth.

Hugh of St. Victor (1100–1141) articulated a
deeper understanding: "When we lift up the eyes of
the mind to what is invisible, we should consider
metaphors of visible things as if they were steps to
understanding." The labyrinth is a visible thing
that, through metaphor, allows us to lift up the eyes
of the mind to the invisible world.

The Chartres Labyrinth

The Chartres labyrinth was laid into the cathedral floor sometime between the Great Fire of
1194 and 1220 when the Fulbert section of the
cathedral was completed. "Scarlet," the cathedral's

first architect, is sometimes credited with introducing the design though his work at Chartres Cathedral, but it predates the physical creation of the labyrinth. Because this labyrinth is one of the few left intact, and is for the most part undamaged, many people think it is the original labyrinth. It is not, but it is one of the last remaining from its time.

The labyrinth is located in the west end of the nave, the central body of the cathedral. When you walk in the main doors and look toward the high altar, you see the center of the labyrinth on the floor about fifty paces in front of you. It is approximately 42 feet in diameter and the path is 16 inches wide. The total walking path is 861.5 feet in length. Unfortunately, because it is covered with chairs many people who have visited Chartres have not even noticed it. A lucky few have reported finding it cleared of chairs for cleaning, and were able to walk it.

Despite the chairs, you can still see the center of the labyrinth which lies in the center aisle of the cathedral. It is a circle about nine feet in diameter with six discernible petals. At Chartres, the center looks like a large scar in the floor. The original centerpiece of the labyrinth was made of copper, brass, and lead. It was removed during the Napoleonic Wars and used as cannon fodder.

Keith Critchlow believes that the center of the Chartres labyrinth had an engraving of the Minotaur, a reference to the Cretan labyrinth on Mount Knossos. For a long time this did not feel right to me. At first I wondered why the Minotaur, a figure from a pre-Christian Greek myth, would appear in the center of the labyrinth in a Christian cathedral. During the flowering of the Middle Ages the church was open to many images and symbols. The Minotaur was incorporated into the Christian teachings as the devil or what we might call a shadow figure. The Christians had to encounter evil forces on the narrow path to good. The Minotaur was encountered and overcome in the center of the labyrinth, and enlightenment was symbolically attained. The Holy Spirit was seen as Ariadne's thread which guided the seeker through the labyrinth of life. When I learned that the name of the Minotaur was Asterion, which means "Star," I understood the Minotaur as a shadow figure that Christianity could embrace.

There are other theories about the original center of the Chartres labyrinth. Some believe that Theseus was pictured, slaying the Minotaur. Others report that Daedalus was engraved in the center, possibly along with the nine now nameless architects of the cathedral. We may never know because the historical records of Chartres from this period have been lost or destroyed.

The Parts That Make the Whole

The Path The singular path of the classical eleven-circuit labyrinth lies in eleven concentric circles with a twelfth being the center of the labyrinth. The path meanders throughout the whole circle. There are thirty-four turns on the path going in to the center.

Six of these are semi-right-angle turns, and twenty-eight others are 180-degree U-turns. The number 12 is important in the sacred arts. It is the multiple of 3, representing heaven, and 4, representing earth. The path over all represents creation.

The Center The center of the labyrinth is often called the rosette. It is made up of a six-petaled rose-shaped area, though traditionally a rose has only five petals. The rose is a symbol for the Virgin Mary, the Mother of God. The Notre Dame cathedrals throughout Europe celebrate her presence. During the High Middle Ages the rose was recognized because of its association with Percival and the Grail myths which flourished during this time. The rose was a sign of beauty and love that dates as far back as the Egyptian myth of Isis and Aphrodite and Venus of classical times.

The Cistercians, through Saint Bernard of Clairvaux (who was a mentor to Hildegard of Bingen in the twelfth century), elevated the status of the Blessed Virgin Mary. They instituted the practice of intercessionary prayers to her, frequently referring to her as the Rose of Sharon. Cowan notes that "the rose becomes symbolic of both human love and Divine Love, of passionate love, but also of love beyond passion." The single rose became a symbol of a simple acceptance of God's love for the world.

The rose, and its Eastern equivalent, the lotus, are almost universally regarded as symbols of enlightenment even today. Both images occur within the context of flowers and cosmic wheels. And according to the historian Rene Guenon, this imagery

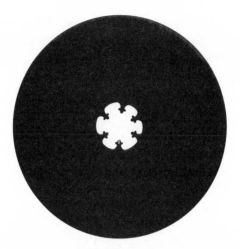

The Petals

was widespread, from Japan, India, and China to Europe well before Christian times.

In the mystical tradition, the rose is a symbol for the Holy Spirit. The six petals in the center symbolize the six days of creation. At Chartres Cathedral, the center of the rose window mirrors the center of the labyrinth. The cathedral is perfectly proportionate, so that if we put the west wall of the cathedral on hinges and folded it down on the labyrinth, the rose window would fit almost perfectly over the labyrinth.

In the cosmic realm, the center can symbolize both the earth and the sun. Jung said the sun was the image of transformation. And Christians see the center representing the Son as well as the sun.

The center can also be understood to symbolize the evolutionary process of Spirit coming into matter. According to Keith Critchlow, each petal of the rose symbolizes one of the six stages of planetary evolution. Starting on the left as you enter the center, the first petal is mineral, then vegetable, animal, human, angelic, and Unknown. When I am in the center of the labyrinth I "visit" each of these petals. I pause to honor and bring into my being first the mineral consciousness, then the vegetable, then animal, human, and angelic. Finally I come to rest in the consciousness of the Unknown, which is the mystery, the divine pattern of evolution that is unfolding and is beyond the grasp of the human mind.

The Labyrs There are ten labyrs in the classical eleven-circuit labyrinth. They are the double-ax symbol visible at the turns, found between the turns throughout the pattern. Labyrs is believed to be the root word of the word labyrinth. They are traditionally seen as a symbol of women's power and creativity. When you look at the pattern as a whole from above, they form a large cross, a cruciform.

The Lunations Lunations are the outer ring of partial circles that completes the outside circle of the labyrinth. They are unique to the classical eleven-circuit labyrinth in Chartres Cathedral. The lunations consist of 28½ two-thirds circles (foils) per quadrant, and therefore 28 cusps (points) per quadrant. The four quadrants of the labyrinth mark each quarter of a year. There is a total of 113 cusps and 112 foils; 1 cusp and 2 foils are absent in the design at the entrance. Some believe that the labyrinth served as a calendar. It offered a method of keeping track of the lunar cycles of twenty-eight days each.

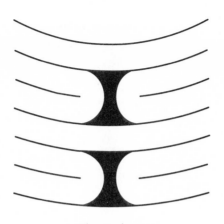

The Labyrs

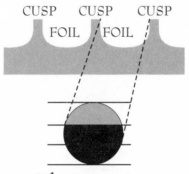

The Lunations

Cusps and Foils

Using this, the church could determine the date of the lunar feast of Easter.

Unfortunately, when people reproduce the Chartres labyrinth design the lunations are often left off. I have come to appreciate and honor the lunations. They add beauty to the labyrinth design and invite us, symbolically, to be back in touch with the lunar cycles. To include them in the making of a labyrinth takes more work, but it does add beauty and power. It completes the sense of the whole cosmos that the Chartres labyrinth conveys. I have been in labyrinths where there were simply decorative lines in place of the lunations. Walking into such a labyrinth felt like walking into a tin can with no resounding energy. When the lunations are left off a labyrinth based on the Chartres labyrinth, I wonder if the creator is unconsciously repeating what we have done over the ages: disregarding the feminine.

This aside, one thing is certain: If the labyrinth you are using does not have the lunations, then it is not a replica of the Chartres labyrinth. Perhaps the lunations are not as important when the labyrinth is a temporary one, made in sand or taped on the floor. But workshop canvases or any form of permanent labyrinth should include the lunations if at all possible.

The lunations are difficult to measure and draw. But without them the power of the labyrinth is reduced and an important layer of meaning is dismissed. The energetic climate of the labyrinth is altered in a way that may make the transmission of images less clear, feelings less distinct, and kinesthetic and sensory experience more difficult to decipher.

The Invisible Thirteen-Pointed Star

Perhaps the most important part of the labyrinth is the invisible thirteen-pointed star that radiates from its center. As you look at the diagram, notice that

The 13 Pointed Star

the points of the star connect the outer lunations
with the center. Two of the lines of the star intersect
directly in the middle of the labyrinth (this point is
at the center of the right-hand path). The crossing
of these lines determines where the petals will be
placed.

On my first trip to Chartres Cathedral we took
detailed measurements of the labyrinth. We thought
these could be easily transferred to our canvas. However, once we got home we realized we did not have
the same amount of space available for our
labyrinth. We would have to transpose the numbers
proportionally. This would have been hard enough,
but when we laid the canvas out on the floor to

begin drawing, we could not get the center right. It would not settle down into anything that looked balanced or symmetrical in relationship to the path. I called Richard Feather Anderson, a dowser and geomancer, who provided wonderful support for the Grace Cathedral labyrinth. He introduced me to the invisible thirteen-pointed star that guides the placement of the path in relationship to the center. I realized there was much more to this than met the eye.

With the help of the star, we were able to place the center properly. Then all the rest of the labyrinth fell into place. After that we developed the labyrinth Seed Kit which is available through Grace Cathedral to help other groups make labyrinths of their own.

The number 13 most likely comes from the Pythagorean ratios that were used to lay out Chartres. It is a prime number, only divisible by itself and the number 1. It is therefore an irreducible expression of the Prime Mover found in Greek thought. In some derivations of numerology, 13 is the number of Christ—12 plus 1. The number 13 is also symbolic of the thirteen full moons in a year. A labyrinth walker turns toward the center thirteen times during the walk.

I believe the invisible star empowers the labyrinth in some inexplicable way. It establishes the pattern for the flow of energy that allows the seeker to have solid and integrative experiences. I have walked classical eleven-circuit labyrinths that were drawn in a linear fashion, without the guidance of the star, and they were not as powerful or centered as they could have been.

An Ancient
Map of the Cosmos

In researching the labyrinth, it doesn't take long to find your way into books naming the paths for the planets. The Chartres labyrinth articulates an ancient cosmology, much as the medicine wheel does for Native American culture. Keith Critchlow believes the source of labyrinth cosmology is most likely from Macrobius's *Commentary on Cicero's Dream of Scipio*. This book was known to have been in the library at the School of Chartres before the cathedral was built. According to the theory, the earth was at the center of the labyrinth. The consecutive circle of paths held the moon, the sun, Mercury, Venus, Mars, Jupiter, and Saturn. The three outermost paths represented the powers of Soul (World Soul), Mind, and Supreme God. Understood in Neoplatonic as well as Christian terms, the person who chooses to walk the labyrinth is "reenacting the descent of the soul" into manifestation on earth (at the center). This moves the seeker through the levels of personality eventually to reflect "the One when it started to fall into differentiation" as well as reflection on Mind and Soul.

Upon entering the labyrinth, we sense that it is a symbol representing the whole. Our world of splits and divisions disappears for a few contented minutes. The seeker enters a nondualistic world, where clear thinking through the channel of intuition has a chance to emerge from deep within. This awareness of the whole facilitates "both/and thinking,"

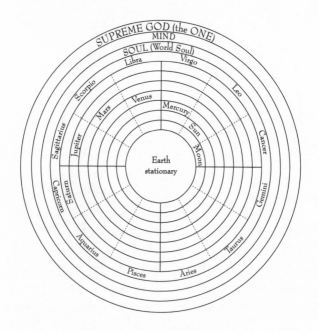

Cicero's Cosmology

the compatibility of paradox and a sense of the unity within the cosmos.

With the shift to Cartesian thought, the labyrinth fell into disuse. This map of the cosmos, with the earth at its center, was discredited. In our drive to embrace the new religion of empirical science, the value of this ancient tool was dismissed. Yet the tool itself remained intact through the centuries.

The Spiral Circle

When walking the labyrinth, you can feel that powerful energies have been set in motion. The labyrinth functions like a spiral, creating a vortex in its center. The path into the center of the labyrinth winds in a clockwise pattern, and the path back unwinds counterclockwise. The spiral is a basic form in nature—although the labyrinth spiral is more complex. The circular path inward cleanses and quiets us as it leads us in. The unwinding path integrates and empowers us on our walk back out. Walking out of the winding path, we are literally ushered back out into the world in a strengthened condition. The cusps, or points, of the lunations serve as conduits for the energy to circulate and radiate outward. People often describe their labyrinth experience in terms of energy: "The center is really powerful tonight," or, "I was drawn to one spot, so I stopped and meditated there for a while."

The labyrinth is a large, complex spiral circle which is an ancient symbol for the Divine Mother, the God within, the Goddess, the Holy in all of creation. Matriarchal spirituality celebrates the hidden and the unseen. It is often symbolized by the cycles of the moon that guide the growing seasons as well as the inner map of knowing in women. For many of us the feminine aspect of the Divine has been painfully absent from our lives, our spirituality, and our Western culture. The Divine feminine is often the missing piece for which both women and men are searching.

With an Open Heart and Mind

There are layers upon layers of meaning in the ancient tool of the labyrinth. This thumbnail sketch is meant to serve as an introduction to the subject. Much more research needs to be done to understand fully the magnificence of this sacred pattern. In the back of the book a partial list of resources is provided to encourage further reading and research. But the best way to learn about the labyrinth is to walk one—with an open heart and an open mind. Then allow your experiences to guide you.

WALKING THE LABYRINTH: THE PROCESS

Solvitur ambulando . . . It is solved by walking . . .

—*Saint Augustine*

T o serve as a canon at a large urban cathedral is a very stressful job. The boundaries are porous. One moment I may be working with a homeless person and ten minutes later joining the procession into the nave of the cathedral to preach in the eleven a.m. service. I noticed that as my stress level went up, my prayer life slowly evaporated. This is a dangerous sign for anyone, but especially for a priest in a demanding spiritual role. So after many attempts to break this pattern, with only limited success, I talked things over with my spiritual director. I decided to explore other methods.

I came across a story about the spiritual discipline of archery as it is taught in the Zen Buddhist tradition. Learning the art of archery was a path to the center of the Self. Aiming the arrow at the target is in essence aiming it at yourself. So learning the skill of archery is learning the skill of self-discovering. We seek our center of calm, our focused guiding voice and keenness of vision. Mastering the flow of our unruly hands, arms, shoulders, and eyes, working them in a congruent way, can bring us closer to our self. This is the purpose of all spiritual disciplines. Prayer, meditation, even fasting, can create in us an openness, a special kind of broad attention. They can renew our awareness of our grounding and wholeness in the mystery of the Sacred.

In our chaotic Western society, many of us have trouble quieting our minds. The Buddhists call the untamed mind the "monkey mind": thoughts swinging from branch to branch, chattering away without rhyme or reason. When the mind is quieter, we feel peaceful and open, aware of a silence that embraces the universe. Complete quiet in the mind is not a realistic goal for most of us. When attempting a sitting meditation, the task is to disidentify with the thoughts going through our minds. Don't get hooked by the thoughts; let them go. Thomas Keating describes the mind as a still lake. A thought is like a fish that swims through it. If you get involved with the fish ("Gee, what an unusual fish. I wonder what it's called"), then you are hooked on the thought.

Walking the labyrinth does not demand a great amount of concentration in order to benefit from the experience. The sheer act of walking a complicated path—which discharges energy—begins to focus the mind. A quiet mind does not happen automatically. But the labyrinth experience sensitizes us, educates us, and helps us distinguish superficial extraneous thoughts from the "thought" that comes from our soul level and that each of us longs to hear. Many of us are discovering that this is much easier to do when our whole body is moving—when we are walking.

The First Walk

Many people who come to Grace Cathedral simply stumble upon the labyrinth. Others have heard of it and have been waiting for a workshop. Here is part of a letter I received that reflects the experience of someone who came in looking for the labyrinth. It captures the spirit of my own movement from curiosity to skepticism to amazement:

> Dear Labyrinth,
> I walked into Grace Cathedral a very long way from home. It was quiet and holy in the Cathedral, with a half dozen or so folks scattered praying or looking at windows. As I walked

around I saw the Labyrinth. I'd heard of this, from a friend in Anchorage, and so I stood and looked at it.

More than a large part of my mind was making skeptical comments and dismissals, but I thought "nothing ventured, nothing gained" and slipped my shoes off and stepped onto the path.

I was aware, as I walked along, how I slowed down, how everything else faded away except the path, and of the adventure of the thing. There were times when I found myself stopping . . . just stopping and standing. An interesting collection of memories would surface at those times. Sometimes it was like . . . playing a record backwards. There were Light and Dark things going on, the Light of the Path elevated over the dark of the Outline.

It took a very long time and I was semi-aware that I was approaching the Center. As I stepped into the Center, somebody someplace thundered the beginning of a fanfare on the Organ. I stood in the Center and smiled, listening to the thunderous organ . . . and then skipped back down the trail.

It would be nice to walk that Thing with the Cathedral pitch dark, except one tall candle burning in the Center.

My apologies to you and Chartres for my skepticism.

Nurturing ourselves spiritually is not an easy thing to do in a culture that disconnects us from our depths. The simple act of walking the labyrinth invites us back into the center of our being. The walk can cause mild anxiety at first, or we may experience fear about what our experience will be. Most often it calms us and guides us. In the end, the turns in the path mirror the turns in our lives. One woman wrote:

Turning Point: The turns in the labyrinth enlightened me to the "turning points" in my life . . . my current one is caring for a seventy-eight-year-old uncle post-operatively. I was forgetting the cumulative effects of drugs/age/helplessness and reacting to some of his unkindly statements. Now recognizing those as he regains his independence, I am able to "turn" from the stings of the words to recognize this need to assert himself. I pray for an improved relationship with him. So glad to be able to meditate with the sacred walk!

The labyrinth is particularly helpful to those of us in transition who are chilled by the winds of change. It also gives solace to those struggling with painful life experiences, like this woman:

Our son is a drug addict. During the last six years we encountered many challenges and through some sort of blind faith we managed to survive all the ups and downs. The crisis we are in at this moment seems insurmountable. And yet we still continue to seek a solution. . . .
    I entered Grace Cathedral feeling as if I were some sort of foreigner. I thought about my religious

experiences as a child growing up as the daughter of a minister. I never quite grasped the concept of religion and drifted away from any kind of church affiliation at age nineteen. It didn't seem right to be in a church. . . .I sat for several minutes trying to reach some conscious contact with a higher power. . . . but it didn't feel right. I decided it couldn't hurt to give the labyrinth a try.

I removed my shoes and hesitated a moment at the entrance. I felt self-conscious as I walked through the first section—as if I were being watched and judged. I concentrated on my breath. As I approached the center I realized that I had entered the labyrinth with some expectations and they didn't seem to be happening. I wanted an-swers to my problems. I wanted some sign that everything would be okay with my family. I wanted guidance as to how to handle my son. I began to feel desperate, almost in tears, as if this was just another phase of my journey through life that would end in another "Oh well, I tried that now. What next?" I tried to clear my mind in anticipa-tion of receiving some sudden lightning bolt of en-couragement. My mind seemed blocked.

As I came to the center of the labyrinth I real-ized that I would not get the solutions to my prob-lems today. I did however feel a sense of peace. As I walked out from the center, I reflected a moment on why I felt peaceful. Two words came to my mind—words that I find very difficult to use: God and Love. It is as if I will be judged for my beliefs

and so am afraid to try to seek what they mean to
me. Could I be scared of my own spirituality? I
am confused but feel I have a new opportunity. I
intend to walk the labyrinth again.

Whatever your situation, the last paragraph of
this letter touches on an important point. There are
no easy solutions to life's many difficult problems.
Yet walking the labyrinth imparts peace. The walk
can also begin a process of insight so a "new opportunity" can come into our awareness.

Small miracles can happen in the labyrinth. We
can strengthen ourselves by shedding tears, feeling
the anger and hurt that keep us from experiencing
our soul level. We can decide that we have held on to
revenge too long, and take action to heal our hateful
feelings. We can reconcile ourselves, perhaps even
with the dead. This woman walked the labyrinth at a
workshop in Colorado:

As I stood waiting my turn to enter the labyrinth,
I began to weep. I had no idea why. I still had no
idea why as I walked, overcome by periodic waves
of weeping, nor did I have any insight as I fin-
ished my walk. As I got outside, however, I sud-
denly felt as if my older sister was talking to me,
and realized that I was in the midst of a healing.
Here's the story.

Years ago, my sister was a dance student at
Colorado College. While I don't particularly associ-
ate the dance studio with her, she surely spent a
great deal of time, for close to eight years, in the

room where the labyrinth was placed. She died of cancer fourteen years ago.

The last time I saw her alive, she laid a "deathbed wish" on me, one that she and I both knew I could not honor. Although we parted without rancor, there was definite strain between us. While I truly understood that she was dying a slow, horrible, premature death and was trying to set her worlds right before she was gone, I mildly resented her asking me to do something which she knew I could not, in good conscience, do. The annoyance, however, was let go of (at least, so I thought) many years ago, and I haven't thought of it, or her, for quite a long time.

My sense today, however, is that my sister came to me with the labyrinth. She seemed to have been waiting there for me in that room, and wanted me to know that she was sorry for having both judged me unfairly and for having placed a burden on me as she died. The sorrow and the tears I experienced were apparently more hers than mine. She asked me for my forgiveness . . . which was easy for me to give, since I'd understood what was going on even at the time. But for a few minutes this morning, out in the sunshine, it was as if we two sisters spoke quietly with one another, healed old hurts, and parted in peace.

Most of the experiences that occur in the labyrinth are unexpected. They are guided by a sacred wisdom, a creative intelligence that knows more about what we need than do our conscious selves.

A Process Meditation

People on the labyrinth seem to gravitate toward what I have come to call a process meditation. This meditation moves between silence and image, so the focus does not remain solely on quieting the mind as in a contemplative practice. This meditation also uses what is very close to a guided imagery process as a source of revelation. We enter the terrain of memory and dreams. But our eyes are open in this receptive, nonjudgmental state, and we can receive whatever arises within us. It is as if we are reading a letter from a beloved but long-lost friend. We move out of chronos time into kairos time, from clock time into dreamtime. In this state of open attention we can again be guided by the movement, through releasing, receiving, and taking back out in the world.

Stepping out of the linear mind is often the most challenging part of the walk. Even though the person has been assured that the path leads to the center, someone who does not surrender easily to experience might stop walking during the first part, trying visually to figure out where the path goes. Of course, there is no right or wrong way to walk the path. This can be a valuable lesson about control and surrendering to process. When a group of people walk the labyrinth, you can find support for dropping deeply within, continuing simply to put one foot in front of the other. Tears of sorrow and what I call "latent" joy frequently arise. People experience a sense of coming home.

The second phase of process meditation symbolically begins in the center but may begin anytime the mind is quiet enough to get beyond itself. We must be open to receive. This is true in life, and we are reminded of it again in the labyrinth. In the space of the labyrinth, we can feel our fear as well as our yearning.

There is a creative tension between allowing images, memories, and feelings to emerge and guiding them through a gentle, gracious, open, and expanded thought process. At the same time, we cannot let our ego get in the way of what is emerging from the soul level.

The walk out of the labyrinth is realistically and symbolically the act of taking what we have received out into the world. This is an empowering and integrating part of the walk. We can honor what has happened in the labyrinth. We may only have a vague sense of the emotions stirring in us, like the woman who reconciled with her sister. Other times we may have a clear sense of what has come to fruition.

One woman who was in an unsatisfying new relationship, a year after her estranged husband died, reported such an experience:

A *few days before I walked the labyrinth this time, I'd had the "head" insight that I wasn't ever going to be happy in a relationship with a man until I learned to love myself. Now saying that I should love myself is a completely different thing than feeling it. As I walked, I began to catalog the reasons I "should" love myself. I'm an accomplished, creative professional. I'm a good mother. I'm this. I'm that. Quite suddenly, as I approached the center, I felt myself swoon (that's the only word I can think of). The words, "I love myself" came to me. No ifs, ands, buts. No conditions. On the way out of the labyrinth that day, I began to think of my "action" in the world as attitude. I could carry on my daily life with a person I loved, me. I could do for me the things I would do for a person I loved. This wasn't so much making a list of "to dos" but a different and incredibly freeing perspective.*

Basic Approaches to the Walk

I suspect there are as many ways to walk the labyrinth as there are people on this planet. The labyrinth can appear quite awesome at first, especially at Grace Cathedral. I want to share these simple guidelines that evolved as I presented the labyrinth to various groups.

What seems to work best when preparing to walk the labyrinth is to take a moment to reflect on where you are in your life. You may want to capture perspective by writing down the parameters that contain your life at that moment. Something as simple as: "Finishing school this May! A job! What am I doing? Kids?" This will help you get your bearings. You may want to focus on a question, or find a statement that guides you to embrace a question or prayer on the labyrinth.

Gracious Attention One approach is simply to quiet the mind, choosing to let all thoughts go when they present themselves in your awareness. In this form of walking the labyrinth, the task is to allow a gracious sense of attention to flow through you. You may find tears welling up, or a sense of peace. Your soul may want to be still and rest.

Asking a Question A second approach to the walk is to focus on a question that we have been asking ourselves. Most of us carry questions subliminally. We are looking for clues to life's puzzles, even if we don't realize it. Part of the preparation for your labyrinth walk can be to bring these questions into your conscious mind.

In workshops, I encourage participants to journal their thoughts before they walk or to share what they are looking for with another participant. The listener may then suggest the unspoken questions that he or she can hear. This gives focus and a context in which to hear from the still, small voice within. In this form of process meditation, it is beneficial to amplify the question and the thoughts surrounding it. Really get into it, look at it from all angles, let all else go but your question. Our intentions guide the process.

Questions that we take into the labyrinth should be outside the realm of yes and no answers. There is nothing magical about the labyrinth. It simply allows our consciousness to open so that deeper, and perhaps new, parts of ourselves can speak to us more directly. The questions that we formulate should be as close to home as possible. They do not need to be worded articulately, but they need to be asked from the heart and soul of our being, not from our everyday conscious thoughts. When people come to the labyrinth at Grace Cathedral, I find they often already have a sense of their question. It may be a burden they are carrying or a decision they are needing to make.

The Use of Repetition Many of us meditate by repeating a word, a mantra, or a phrase over and over to ourselves. There are at least two different theories as to what kind of phrases to use. Those who have learned the contemplative method of Christian centering prayer have been advised to use a word or phrase that does not stir up either positive or negative feelings or thoughts. A word from another language or even a nonsense phrase can accomplish this. Thomas Keating suggests short words such as *Abba*, which means "Father" in Aramaic, but this can still be a loaded word for many. This approach distracts the restless mind by keeping it busy.

The other approach is to find a meaningful phrase—which lends itself nicely to the walk. I use different phrases depending upon what I need at the time. I invite the Holy Spirit into my life. "Come Holy Spirit, come." Sometimes I remind myself that I am part of the Light. I might say, "I am a daughter of the Light," or "Help me God, to remember I am a daughter of the Light." Other times I may just say, "Guide me, Mother of God."

A meditation in the Buddhist tradition, written by Stephen Levine, can be repeated silently within the heart. It is especially good for people who are in a healing process:

> May I dwell in the heart
> May I be free from suffering
> May I be healed
> May I be at peace

These prayerful phrases are similar to affirmations and the more they make sense in your internal experience, the more helpful they are. This method still focuses the mind, but it attempts to engage it rather than distract it. Try experiencing the results of both methods to determine which one works best for you. A man wrote to me after a workshop:

> When I said, at the start of the day, that I was looking for something to invigorate my arid prayer life, I had no idea how helpful walking the labyrinth would be. I came away with a renewed appreciation for the ordinariness of my life. I have a much better understanding that the sacred path is, literally and figuratively, a pedestrian path, complete with all the jerky starts and unexpected bumps and stops that occur in our daily lives.

Reading Scripture Traditionally in Christianity, there are three ways of getting to know God. The first is through given knowledge, like the Scriptures. The second is through traditions such as liturgical worship and spiritual writings of those who have lived within the tradition before us. The last is through continued revelation or direct experience of the Holy. The third avenue has always been controversial, and depending on the denomination or the tradition, comes with all kinds of caveats. I think it is pretty clear how walking the labyrinth might enhance the third way of knowing God. However, the labyrinth can also be used as a way to deepen our understanding and experiences of the first two. For example, a woman who was fascinated by the labyrinth had been taught that we know God only through Scripture. She asked permission to read the Psalms. I loaned her a Book of Common Prayer. She read it as she walked, moving slowly through the labyrinth in order to follow the path. In the center she sat and read her favorite Psalm, then closed her eyes to pray.

And of course, one could read other books on spirituality while walking the labyrinth. While it is slightly different, I'm reminded of monastic communities that practice *lectio divina* during mealtimes, when a designated reader reads aloud to the community from spiritual classics.

Asking for Help through Prayer Another method is simply to pray throughout the labyrinth walk. A teacher walking the labyrinth found that thoughts of each of her students came to mind. As she prayed for them by name, she saw each of their faces. If something is weighing heavily on your mind and heart, the labyrinth can give you enormous support. You might simply want to talk to God, as if you were writing a letter: "Dear God" or "Dear Divine Mystery, I need to speak to you . . ." A young boy walked the labyrinth through the Chrysalis group in Richmond, Virginia. When he finished the labyrinth, he went to his mother and asked if he could do it again. She gave him permission and asked why. He told her, "I think I was talking to God, and the conversation is not over yet." The labyrinth is a sacred space where we can talk to God.

One of the things we forget most easily is to ask for help from the Divine. What do we need? This is a question to ask ourselves every day, and especially when we are approaching a labyrinth. To ask is to nurture ourselves spiritually. The labyrinth is a place where you can pour your heart out, express your anger, experience joy, express gratitude—and perhaps above all, ask for what you need.

Honoring a Benchmark in Time

Many people walk the labyrinth to honor a benchmark in time. It may be a birthday or the anniversary of a close friend's death. We can walk the labyrinth to pray for a person who is undergoing surgery or to support and sustain a board of leaders making an important decision.

When we opened the labyrinth to the public, a group of musicians called Musica Divina came to play and sing at the labyrinth. The men and women in this group had a revered Sufi teacher named Hayat Stadlinger. One night Hayat came to hear them play and, although she hadn't planned to, she walked the labyrinth. At ninety-two years of age, she is probably the oldest person to have walked the labyrinth. She returned two other times. Though she was quite frail, she never needed assistance because she was sturdy and determined. Knowing that Hayat was special to many people, I granted permission for her followers to videotape her when she walked the labyrinth amid the many people who came to the third Wednesday evening event. When Hayat died I felt sweet sorrow. A friend wrote:

> The memorial for Hayat Stadlinger was held outside because the hundreds of people who came couldn't all fit in the house at once. Her house was open and filled with candles and flowers. The video of Hayat walking the Labyrinth as Musica Divina played was being run in her bedroom—the place where she passed over. Seeing that video gave me a deep sense of continuum, of history. This remarkable woman had walked a path that I was still treading—that all lovers of beauty have been walking since we appeared on the earth. I was comforted seeing my darling Hayat walking that timeless symbol—the Labyrinth—the returning path to the Beloved.

A Body Prayer

Many of us are shy when it comes to movement. But in the container of the labyrinth there is support for moving spontaneously as our body wishes. The structured nature of the path seems to encourage this. It provides a safe feeling of containment. At the beginning of workshops I encourage people to move as they wish. It is important to follow the impulses that arise within us. Some people may chant, others may dance, cry, or laugh out loud. Sometimes friends greet each other with a hug. Using the gift of our breath is not only a way into clearing our minds, it is a way through the anxiety, self-consciousness, or uncertainty that we may feel while we are on the labyrinth.

During workshops that are musically reinforced, people are even better able to experience the flow their body seeks. Some people dance, others skip or crawl. One woman became like an inchworm, moving herself through the labyrinth by extending and contracting her body. I provide colorful scarves of different sizes for people to use as they wish. Some dance with them; others place them over their heads so they can "hide" as they go deeply within.

Insights in the labyrinth are not always received verbally. One can sense something on the kinetic level that defies words. One friend of mine frequently experiences an opening of the Hara, a stream of energy moving through her body that begins in the abdomen, in the center of the labyrinth. This experience helps her feel more grounded, more alive in her body. A sister in a religious order wrote to me after a day-long retreat.

As I walked the fields yesterday, I was once again reminded of the labyrinth walk, a wonderful experience to say the least. I am so much more aware of the importance of body as well as mind and spirit in maintaining a healthy balance in all areas of our life. Including all three aspects of ourselves in prayer is so powerful! Something synergistically mysterious happens for me when I apply body-mind-spirit to prayer. The labyrinth is a very simple (as in easy to do, not easy-to-comprehend) way to achieve that goal.

Over the years that I have been presenting the labyrinth to the public we have had a number of people with disabilities walk the labyrinth. Wheelchairs work just fine on the labyrinth. Usually it is more meditative for the person in a wheelchair if someone else guides him or her through the labyrinth, because he or she can relinquish control without having to be concerned about moving through and around people.

Sometimes people who can walk will not have enough stamina to go the whole distance, nearly a third of a mile, all at one time. When this is the case, I usually keep an eye on them and when they want to sit, they give me a signal and I will walk in with a chair for them to sit on and rest wherever they are.

For visually challenged persons, we have developed a finger meditation tool. This is an eighteen-by-eighteen-inch pattern. The edges are raised so the finger is guided along the path. When someone can't see, it is helpful to have an overview of the labyrinth before he or she is led onto it. This meditation tool is a great way to achieve that.

Allowing the Ego to Let Go

When you walk the labyrinth, one of the first things you may notice is an internal voice. It may be chiding you to do the walk differently, or willing the person ahead of you to move faster because you don't feel right going around him or her. Stepping into the labyrinth, we see our thoughts for what they are. We may meet the impatient, judgmental thoughts that are so much a part of us that we no longer notice them. One of the major reasons we need a spiritual practice is to get beyond the ego, the manager of our personality.

When we are able to see through or step beyond the ego, the outside world becomes a mirror that reflects what we are seeking. The people and events in our lives become part of our path, part of the invisible thread that leads onward. We feel surrounded by the Holy. And all the pain and joy that we experience tempers us, allows us clearly to see our struggling, suffering world. It is difficult to accept that we are living on a dying planet. But once we experience the grief, we can become wise leaders and agents of change.

If we are struggling with the ego, the method of gracious attention may have fewer pitfalls. We simply present ourselves as ready to release whatever comes up in us, and to receive what awaits us in the center. Focusing on a question can be an invitation to involve the ego, which often stops the flow of images. The ability to differentiate between flow and force on the ego level is important. The human ego can attempt to force something out of its own timing, and then we come up empty. "Don't push the river . . . it flows by itself" is a good philosophy for the labyrinth.

When we know ourselves well, we know how our thoughts try to shape things. Expectations often get in the way of our experience. I offered the labyrinth walk at a friend's family gathering. Their college-age son expected to go to the center and get "shazammed." When this did not happen, he was disappointed. But when his father walked out of the labyrinth a few minutes later, in emotional turmoil, the son then realized that his own expectations had limited his experience.

This can happen to anyone, and it is part of gaining self-knowledge. If we take a walk in the country expecting to see a frog, our whole walk can be so focused on finding the frog that we miss the beauty of the countryside. If we do find the frog, we miss learning how our expectations shape our world around us. But this rarely works in life. Expectations cut us off from the flow of life and set us up for disappointment.

The mind can play tricks on us in the center of the labyrinth as well. Most commonly, it may deny us the nugget of information we have been searching for. In *Wild Mind*, a book about developing the skill of writing, Natalie Goldberg talks about getting to "first thoughts." We want the original zany, creative thought. But often when it comes, the critic in our minds may not be able tolerate it. The thought may be too original, too creative, too ugly or mysteriously fragmented. Thus it is denied, masked, forgotten—and never walks out of the labyrinth with us.

Assigning premature meaning to insights we receive in the center of the labyrinth is another trick the mind can play on us. I presented the labyrinth to a group of seminary students. One woman in her mid-twenties walked to the center and felt a flash of elation. Then she had a strong image of her mother, with the association of death or dread. She discussed this with me, fearing that it might mean that her perfectly healthy mother would suddenly die. Since it was a Lenten Quiet Day, we had the privilege of sorting this out in stages throughout the day. We talked together after each of the three times she walked the labyrinth. By the end of the day, she had become aware that most of her actions were punctuated by the thought "What would my mother think?" She was enjoying seminary a great deal, hence the elation. But her mother was raised in a very conservative tradition and disapproved of a woman having a theological education. This produced the feeling of dread within her. Her initial fear that her mother was going to die may have clouded her deeper understanding of the psychological and spiritual work she needed to do. She needed to free herself from her mother's judgments. By the end of the day she saw this issue clearly.

Working with Dreams

Dreams are not strangers to me. Years of psychotherapeutic work, as client and therapist, have taught me respect for the revelations of my unconscious. After working with the labyrinth for about a year, I had a rare moment alone with it in the gymnasium at the Kanuga Conference Center in North Carolina. A dream from the night before was weighing on my mind, so I decided to hold it in focus as I walked the labyrinth. The tiny visual image that remained embedded in my inner eye began to take on a life of its own. It changed shape and began to move, association through association. I found myself on the streets of Prague, in a place where I had actually been the summer before, reliving a joyous moment. Never before had the process of discovery flowed so naturally for me as on the labyrinth.

One man dreamed of preparing to attend an important budget meeting. In the dream, when it came time for the meeting he was in the next room taking a nap. He woke up forty-five minutes after the meeting began, and went into the conference room, where everyone was intensely focused on numbers written on a blackboard. No one noticed him and he couldn't find a place to sit down. Finally someone shared the numbers with him, telling him, "It doesn't look good." On the labyrinth the dreamer was able to feel through the specifics of the dream. He realized this dream was a wake-up call for him. In actuality, he had been removing himself from the budgeting process at his company at a time when he needed to be attentive. At the time of the dream he thought the planning for the next year would be fine. But when he arrived back at work, it turned out that indeed it didn't look good.

The spiritual transformation we are undergoing demands that we stop ignoring our own internal wisdom. Dreams, myths, stories, and insight through the imagination need to come back into the mainstream of our personal and collective awareness. They are avenues of inspiration and action for the transformation to occur. Even when dreams may serve as a way to discover revelations in sacred stories, we tend to dismiss their value. Our bodies are cut off from our minds, and our minds are cut off from our evolving consciousness. The vision of unity, the wholeness of creation, has been lost. To create and make new we need access to the field of collective imagination that speaks to us from a unifying Source. We need to communicate with the choreographer of creation to hasten personal integration and spark collective vision. We need to find our field of dreams.

In June 1994 I returned to Kanuga Conference Center to take part in a conference called Ancient Spiritual Paths: Soul Making, the Labyrinth and the Dream. After an initial introduction on the significance of the labyrinth and how to walk it, we opened the labyrinth with a ritual and left it open around the clock for the whole week. There was music available if participants wanted to turn on the sound system. The labyrinth provided a place for contemplation, reflection, and ritual. One woman wrote to me recently about her experience. She had had a powerful dream a month before the conference:

I had found this dream rather painful and frustrating, but I had really not thought past the literal circumstances. But the labyrinth kept bringing it

back up for me, nagging me almost, and I took
that for an indication that I needed to get into the
deeper levels of it.

During the conference, she began to discuss the
dream in her group and to walk the labyrinth to reflect on it. Throughout the presentations, labyrinth
walking, and group meetings she began to hear
pieces of insight from others that gave her significant clues to unraveling the dream:

The last night having come to an interpretation
that felt true, I went to the labyrinth with the clear
intention of making peace with these buried parts
of myself. The whole room was just full of currents
that evening, with people reaching out to one an-
other in the most loving and natural ways, and the
spiritual power was almost palpable. I felt as if the
understanding and the healing that came from
confronting the dream were a gift the labyrinth led
me to.

Back in the mundane world, I am still draw-
ing nourishment, writing in ways I have been un-
able to do about deeper subjects and with a new
comfort about taking self-revealing risks in my po-
etry and my relations with other people. I hope
there will soon be a labyrinth in every city—at
least one! It's hard not to proselytize and be tire-
some to the uninitiated.

Working with a dream on the labyrinth is another form of process meditation. The guideline is

to keep opening up the image that is presented. Then as it opens, we can interact with it, talk to it, and listen to it. We can take a dream directly into the labyrinth, or a dream fragment may simply float to the surface of our awareness. People frequently dream about the labyrinth itself before they walk it. Many then realize the dream when they are on the labyrinth. People also often dream a great deal about the labyrinth experience after they have walked. If a dream comes to our memory during the walk, we need to choose whether or not to pay attention to it, especially if we had planned to use another method of prayer or meditation. Knowing the landscape of our psyches can help us discern what we need to do. I usually honor a dream with my attention if it comes to me on the labyrinth. I feel it must have come for a reason. Perhaps it provides a clue, or a path to a question I am just beginning to ask.

Angels and Other Avenues of Inspiration

Entering the sacred space of the labyrinth can open us to experiences beyond the ordinary. One man wrote me a letter that began, "I want you to know that I was not on any drugs or alcohol at the time of my experience." He went on to describe how he walked into the center of the canvas labyrinth when it was in the cathedral and saw a huge luminous Christ standing there arms out-stretched, inviting the man toward Him.

Many people have reported seeing angels around the labyrinth. And although I rarely see into the invisible world, I often feel a soft and graceful air around the labyrinth. Judith, a friend and leader in the Women's Dream Quest, described her experience:

My most profound journey on the labyrinth occurred during the Women's Dream Quest in 1993. It was the first time we had used the labyrinth as a focal point of our yearly ritual and we had 140 women moving, dancing, dreaming in the cathedral. I had spent the evening giving healings and blessings. My experience was extraordinary. There was a palpable softness, and a feeling of great receptivity with everyone. Hearts were flowing open. I felt especially able to give my gift. It was from this state of awareness that I began my labyrinth walk late at night when most of the women were asleep. I was anticipating going with the labyrinth to Washington the next day for Clinton's inauguration. I was hopeful, grateful, full of love.

I made my way with ease along the curving path. I remember feeling light, praying prayers of gratefulness to all the spirits that we had called on during our ritual. When I arrived in the center a strong feeling of awe sent me to my knees. I saw in a way that I have only seen maybe a dozen times in my life. First I saw a shimmering, undulating, configuration of rectangles—vortices of energy above the labyrinth. And then I saw beings of light-blue in hue, faceless but human in form in solemn procession as if on their own labyrinth. They moved in right action dancing their own choreography. I felt wonderful to be sharing the space with these beings—angels, guardians, of the labyrinth.

The labyrinth was a gateway for me into the unseen world that seems to accompany us always. The path, ritually taken, opens and brings me to just where I need to be to access my sight, my knowing, my wisdom.

The Labyrinth as Metaphor

The metaphors within the labyrinth are endless because they are shaped by our creative imaginations. Most immediate are the journey to our center of being and the creation of order from chaos. Completion, competition, emptying, turning our back on the center, distrusting our judgment—whatever our psyches need to deal with becomes the spiritual lesson of the labyrinth.

The labyrinth captures the mystical union between heaven and earth, an understanding of death and rebirth. It is a path of faith and doubt, the complexity of the brain, the turns of the intestine, and the birth canal, and the Celestial City. In medieval times, the labyrinth was said to reflect our entanglements in a deceitful world, unless we allowed God to guide us along the way.

As soon as you get settled into the labyrinth walk and get your bearings, one or more metaphors may spark within. The walk, and all that happens on it, can be grasped through the intuitive, pattern-discerning faculty of the person walking it. The genius of this tool is that it reflects back to the seeker whatever he or she needs to discover from a new level of awareness. When the ego is not tightly engaged in control, it joins the other parts of our being to allow us to see through the moment, to see beyond ourselves into the dynamic that is unfolding before us. This is the gift of being able to see the infinite in the context of the finite. And somehow we are surrounded by a gentle love at the same time.

Experiencing Our Experience

Most people who walk into the labyrinth find peace and have an insightful experience the first time. However, there are a few people who simply do not understand the labyrinth even after walking it more than once. I have observed these people for some time and sense that they are not able to reflect on their experience. The labyrinth is an evocative tool. It works through the imagination and the senses, creating an awareness of how we relate to ourselves, to others, and to the Holy. To reap the benefits of these insights demands that we be able to "experience our experience" in a conscious way. For instance, we can walk into the labyrinth in a judgmental state of mind. We view the crying woman as silly for being so vulnerable and the man who is swinging his arms as he drifts along the path as playacting. The person unable to reflect on his or her own thoughts and feelings will simply end the labyrinth walk in the same frame of mind. However, the reflective person would recognize her thoughts as judgmental. The reflective person would understand that these thoughts curtailed his chance of a deeper connection to himself or others. Realizing this, the person may begin to allow the judgments to dissipate.

Experiencing our feelings and inner thoughts without judgment is part of developing spiritual maturity. In order to reflect, we need a quiet place inside ourselves. It is from this place that we are able to make subtle shifts of attitude when necessary, without condemning ourselves. If we walk on a beach without winding down to breathe in the ocean air, we stay disconnected from a nourishing experience. This can also happen with the labyrinth. The time on the labyrinth is meant to be a reflective and meditative act when you stay in the moment with your experience.

Receptivity

Walking the labyrinth is an act of receptivity, as well as reflection. During intensive bioenergetic work in the 1970s, I learned the difference between a "hard-eye" state and a "soft-eye" state. Hard eyes are for long-distance looking: surveying, seeking, looking ahead. Soft eyes are for up-close, intimate contact. Soft-eye states are gentle: they behold a loved one, or a moment when we are inward with our thoughts and feelings. On the labyrinth, seekers can savor their experience through soft-eye vision. This is where we meet ourselves and catch glimpses of the Divine.

Just as in other forms of meditation, it is possible to have an uneventful experience on the labyrinth. There are times when nothing significant happens, when the timing simply may not be right for anything to emerge. There are benefits to walking it anyway. It is like dreaming: even if you don't remember the dream or are unable to analyze it, it is still beneficial to have dreamed it. Dreams help maintain the psyche's health. If our night dreams are interrupted, we get irritable and unfocused in our daily activities. Over the months that I have been using the labyrinth as a meditation discipline, there seems to be a cumulative benefit. I feel more focused, more spacious within, and more responsive to the people I encounter in my life.

Finding Your Pace

In our chaotic world we are often rushed, pushed beyond a comfortable rhythm. We lose the sense of our own needs. Even worse, we're often rushed and then forced to wait. Anyone who has hurried to the bank only to stand in line knows what I mean. Ironically, the same thing can happen on the labyrinth. But there is a difference—the labyrinth can help us find our natural pace, and draws our attention to the times when we don't honor it.

Waiting on the labyrinth can become a nurturing experience, depending solely on your attitude. Recently, during a monthly program we have at Grace called Taize Around the Labyrinth, there were more than fifty people on the labyrinth at once, chanting as they walked. By the middle of the event there was a line of people waiting to enter the center. Everyone stood patiently on the path and began to chant louder, gently swaying with the music. My hunch is that people enjoy the sense of community that is visible when many walk the labyrinth at the same time. There was a sense of goodwill, a feeling of being bathed in love.

Along with finding your pace, it is important to support your movement through the labyrinth by becoming conscious of your breath. We may have the tendency to hold our breath. Let your breath flow smoothly in and out of your body. It can be co-ordinated with each step if you choose, as in a Buddhist walking meditation. Let your experience be your guide. One meditator said:

Somehow the labyrinth fits right into my Buddhist work. Buddhism has a tradition of walking meditation (kinhin) so it fits nicely. I carry the labyrinth in my mind, so that sometimes at work I can call it up and walk it while I walk down the hall. Very short, but nice.

Each experience in the labyrinth is different, even if you walk it many times over a short period. The pace usually differs each time as well. It can also change dramatically within the different stages of a single walk. You can pass others, in order to honor your intuitive pace. If you are moving at a slower pace, you can allow others to pass you. At first, some people are uncomfortable with the idea of passing someone else on the labyrinth. It seems competitive, especially since the walk is a spiritual exercise. We hope these kinds of feelings can be greeted from a place within that smiles knowingly about the machinations of the human ego. The labyrinth's winding path helps us find our pace, allows us a spaciousness within, encourages our receptivity to and develops our awareness of the habitual thoughts and issues we put in the way of our spiritual development. It is a road to self-knowledge.

Getting Lost in the Labyrinth

The path through the labyrinth is a two-way street. When we meet someone going in the opposite direction, how do we greet, meet, and step around this person? We may choose to step off the path. If the labyrinth is new to us, or if it is crowded, our eyes can be confused by the lines. We may step back into the wrong place and lose our way. This can cause a fair amount of anxiety. But if we do get lost, one of two things can happen: we either return to the center or return to the entrance. And usually we have learned something about ourselves.

I was so absorbed in the process on the way out from the center, that I didn't realize I had lost my way somewhere along the line and ended up back

*in the middle . . . This would usually have caused
me trouble. Ordinarily I would have been so dis-
tracted at doing it wrong that I would have completely lost awareness of what I was supposed to
be doing. Add to that embarrassment, frustration,
irritation . . . well, I suppose you get the picture.
This time, however, I was immediately aware of
the thought that this is exactly what happens to
us when we are on the path of our spiritual journey—when we get lost, God just leads us back to
the center, and it doesn't make a whit of difference
which road gets us there.*

In the labyrinth our life patterns become clear.
One man had a very uncomfortable walk through
the labyrinth during a workshop. He did not feel
free to pass his friend, a serious Buddhist meditator
who walked the labyrinth matching one breath to
one step. Staying behind her, he disregarded his own
pace, his own needs. He found himself getting de-
pressed on the labyrinth. Later, he realized what he
had done. He also recognized that subjugating his
own needs to follow someone he perceived as more
knowledgeable, or as having more authority, had
been a pattern in his life.

If we are impatient or unassertive in life, we will
most likely begin that way in the labyrinth. If we
allow ourselves to evolve with the meditative process,
allowing our first thoughts, we can begin to experi-
ment with new behavior. We can find new ways of
being that our souls longed for us to express. If the
man who remained behind the Buddhist meditator

had found the courage to move around her, his feelings of fear might have been followed by feelings of liberation and relief. My hope is that he visit the labyrinth at another time. To provide this opportunity, we need community groups to come together to create labyrinths in their local areas so people have access to them.

There is no way directly to control the effect that walking the labyrinth will have on us. We can enter with an intention, but may realize that the intention came from our head, not our heart. We may be surprised by tears, joy, or sorrow without any hint that these feelings were lurking in the background of our experience. Over the years, I have learned to trust the uncanny wisdom inspired by the labyrinth. I have become convinced that our lack of control is part of the genius of this tool. A workshop can provide a climate of sacred space and a ritual in which the walk can occur. After that, everyone is very much on his or her own. Any theme may come to our attention while we walk. Our own life experience, our role in the cosmic dance, is the raw material for the sacred ritual of walking the labyrinth.

THE SEEDS
OF SPIRITUAL
HUNGER

Christianity stripped its world of magic and mystery,
and of the possibility of spiritual renewal through
itself . . . It had rendered its people alienated
sojourners in a spiritually barren world where the only
outlet for the urge of life was the restless drive onward.

—*Frederick Turner*

When I was making the decision to move from New York City to San Francisco, I had a significant dream that ended with the line "It's all about the fourteenth century." This sent me scurrying to a copy of Barbara Tuchman's book *A Distant Mirror: The Calamitous Fourteenth Century.* My attention had been in the clinical world for many years, so I had not read a history book since my seminary days. It was a thrill to enter into the world of that century, which mirrors the times of transition we are experiencing at the end of the twentieth century.

It was in the fourteenth century that the structure of the medieval church, which shaped so much of daily life, began to crack and fall away. According to Tuchman, when people ceased to believe that the afterlife was superior to the here and now, the Middle Ages ended and the modern age began. Belief in the afterlife was replaced by "belief in the worth of the individual and of an active life not necessarily focused on God."

We are now ending an age. We are beginning to realize that Western civilization—held together by rationalism, empirical research, and man's control of nature—is coming apart. This is no longer an accurate description of the world in which we live. As we in the West learned to use our rational minds, we developed a sense of superiority that denied our intuition and imagination their rightful place among the human faculties we need to survive.

We lost our sense of connection to ourselves and to the vast mystery of creation that contains other forms of life. The web of creation has been thrown out of balance, so the threat to life on planet Earth looms like storm clouds on the horizon. "From the time of our remote ancestors until the seventeenth century," says Rupert Sheldrake, "it was taken for granted that the world of nature was alive. But in the last three centuries, a number of educated people have come to think of nature as lifeless. This has been the central doctrine of science—the mechanis-

tic theory of nature." This is where we lost the great-
grandmother's thread.

The Cosmos and the Soul

As science became the new religion, the church
held to the old view of the universe. The split
between science and religion also became the split
between the cosmos and the soul. Humans misinter-
preted the biblical injunction that "dominion" over
the earth meant the right to pillage and plunder—to
control natural resources for profit with little con-
sideration for conserving them for the generations
to come. Harold Stone said:

> We live in an age of revolution, a revolution of the
> unconscious, which is destroying old forms and
> often has nothing to substitute for the old ways
> but chaotic energy. We are reaping the harvest of
> centuries of repression of the unconscious. Western
> man has long since destroyed his Gods and substi-
> tuted in their place the gods of Reason and Ratio-
> nality. Imagination has been lost. Emotions have
> been negated. Dreams have become a forgotten
> language. Demons have been ruled out of exis-
> tence, Evil has been consigned to the metaphysical
> constructs of the Middle Ages. We, all of us, are
> both the victims and the processors of this brand
> of insanity, and today we are all paying the piper.
> The unconscious is in revolt against its oppressor;
> namely, rational consciousness as it has been
> known over the past few centuries.

The twelfth and thirteenth centuries, the High Middle Ages, were a prosperous time in Europe. Commerce stimulated advances in every area of life: the establishment of the university system as we know it today, the exploration of the land and surrounding seas. Cities took root and flowered, banking and credit systems developed, and there was an explosion of creativity in art and technology. The compass, the mechanical clock, the spinning wheel, the treadle loom, the windmill and watermill were all invented. The construction of eighty Gothic cathedrals and five hundred churches within a period of a hundred years gave this period its name. Labyrinths were placed in churches and cathedrals throughout France and northern Italy along with the flying buttresses and rose windows that made Gothic architecture unique. The French cathedrals of Chartres, Amiens, Bayeux, and Mirepoix and the Italian cathedrals at Lucca and Santa Marla in Trastavere in Rome all still have labyrinths. Sadly, the labyrinths at Auxerre, Rheims, Poitiers, and many other cathedrals have been destroyed or overlaid.

An esoteric school existed at Chartres Cathedral from the sixth through the twelfth centuries. It integrated neoplatonic thought with Christianity. This school embraced the seven liberal arts and was extremely influential until the University of Paris superseded it around the thirteenth century. In addition to grammar, rhetoric, and dialectics, the scholars at the School of Chartres taught four ways of knowing the world: arithmetic (the science of numbers), geometry (the science of space and how to master it), astronomy (the science of mechanism learned through observation and reflection), and music (the science of universal harmony).

Three central questions asked by scholars of the School of Chartres still challenge us today: How can we, through the connection with the spirit, heal the soul? How can we, working on the Earth, heal our planet? How can we, through a communion in the spirit, heal the body social?

Though a direct connection between the labyrinth and the School of Chartres is not ordinarily made, the labyrinth is based on arithmetic, geometry, astronomy, and music. My hunch is that if the labyrinth was not created by these early geniuses, it was at least protected, utilized, and passed down through the centuries as part of sacred knowledge by these brilliant masters of Spirit.

What was forgotten in our escape to rationalism is now coming back into our collective memory. The seeds planted by the School of Chartres and the great mystics from all traditions have taken root and now greet the light of day. One person who had used the labyrinth over a period of three weeks wrote, "The labyrinth remains a memory which takes me back before my own recorded memory into a sacred past of deep connection to the Holy."

Exploring the Potential of the Labyrinth

Opening the canvas labyrinth in the nave of Grace Cathedral ruffled only a few feathers and piqued the creative imagination of many people. The story of people's labyrinth experiences were passed from friend to friend, teacher to class, family member to family member, group member to group, client to therapist, student to spiritual director. Wherever people were talking about spirituality, they were talking about the labyrinth.

Once the labyrinth was open to the public, I was free to shift my perspective and deepen my approach to this unusual ministry that was taking shape before my eyes. I was reminded of the statement made by geneticist Barbara McClintock when she received the Nobel Prize: "It might seem unfair to reward a person for having so much pleasure over the years asking the maize plant to solve specific problems and then watching its responses." Her insight allowed me to embrace an attitude of observation and participation that was wonderfully expansive.

I had many questions about the use of the labyrinth. Was it a tool for transformation? Did it weave together the psyche and soul that were split so long ago that we barely have memory of it?

We offered the canvas labyrinth to the public twice a month in the nave of Grace Cathedral. During this same period of time I formed two groups that met for six consecutive weeks. Eight to ten people in each group focused on the theme of co-creation, or self-knowledge. One participant—a writer, director, and producer—wrote me over a year later to say, "My time working with co-creation on the labyrinth still stands out as a particularly powerful and productive period, unmatched in most ways since then."

I made it a point to walk the labyrinth as often as possible. Nearly every time I walked it, I took in my questions about the labyrinth itself. I invariably got the same message: "Keep going." My role was to watch, listen, and let people teach me through their experiences. As the Labyrinth Project blossomed into full flower at Grace Cathedral, I began to travel with the labyrinth. My intuition was my guide in structuring the workshops and developing ritual.

I observed people walking the labyrinth and spoke with many of them who were eager to share their experiences. Two distinct characteristics of the labyrinth seemed to emerge: the use of the imagination it engenders and the flow that occurs in the presence of a receptive, feminine approach. Both the imagination and the feminine were devalued when we moved out of the Middle Ages, and in their suppression lie the seeds of our present-day spiritual hunger. They are the missing link that Western civilization needs to reclaim if we are to evolve and meet the challenges of our new civilization that is groaning in birth.

The Imagination in Exile

We have placed the imagination in exile. We have banished it because we do not understand or trust it. Nor do we grasp the imagination's connection to the Divine within. As we stand on the brink of the next century looking back into the mirror of the fourteenth century, we face an odd paradox. During the fourteenth century, the human faculty of the imagination was not empowered by sufficient rationality. Today, the reverse is true. Now rationality is not empowered sufficiently by the imagination. It is almost as if an hourglass has been turned upside down and the sand is flowing the opposite way. William Blake understood this when he said that "the enemy of whole vision is reasoning power's divorce from the imagination." The divorce between the reasoning mind and the imaginative mind places us in peril. The relationship between reasoning and imagination, thought and image, remains divided even in our modern world. The labyrinth can repair this split. The labyrinth can bring the imagination out of exile.

Aristotle said that "the soul thinks in images." It is the experience of soul we hunger for. Dreams, stories, and myths have been relegated to make-believe. They are not honored for their healing and prophetic qualities that have guided human beings through the ages. The mistrust of the imagination is a result of mystical experience being confused with superstition and magical thinking, which is hidden in the shadow side of the church.

In his passionate book *The Waning of the Middle Ages*, J. Huizinga addresses the issue of imagination at the end of the Middle Ages in France and the Netherlands. He brings to his research a fascination with the way the imagination functioned in the medieval mind. Huizinga's work has served as a helpful source in piecing together how mystical experience became confused with superstition and how the imagination was forced into exile.

During the Middle Ages, the church provided an

all-encompassing context for people's lives. From birth to death, the teachings of the church permeated every nook and cranny of human life. The teachings of the church reinforced a fear-filled message, and people lived in submission to the words of the priests—the mediators between man and God. This religious rhetoric flooded the human consciousness through prolific religious imagery as well. Fiery paintings of hell and pastoral paintings of heaven reminded everyone that the goal of this life was to prepare for the next life. Murals lining church walls taught Bible stories to an illiterate population. Christian symbols flourished. The celebration of Christian feast days were high points in an otherwise dreary life for many people.

Pious religious sentiment ran freely, reaching its high point in Lent. Both men and women cried frequently, often in public, and especially during sermons that were often preached in town squares. This was encouraged by the reading of Psalm 42:3: "My tears have been my food day and night."

The imagination of the person in the Middle Ages frequently merged with the image unfettered by rational thought. The rational mind was not developed enough to mediate between unruly images and the conclusions of reason. This placed people at the mercy of their own inner projections, with little ability to discern their experiences. A "poor nun carrying wood to the kitchen imagines she carries the cross; a blind woman doing the washing takes the tub for the manger and the warehouse for the stable." An epileptic woman thought that each "twinge of pain in her corns was a sign that a soul descended to hell."

The experience of the Passion of Christ was burned into the imagination of children. Saint Colette, for example, recalled hearing her mother weep and lament about the Passion every day. This affected her so deeply that throughout her life she felt an oppressive weight on her heart daily at the hour of the crucifixion. And at the reading of the Passion, "she suffered more than a woman in childbirth."

The adoration of relics was vital to the medieval person. Relics that were close to the core of the Christian story—a supposed bone fragment from Saint John the Baptist, or a splinter from Jesus' cross—were often the destinations of pilgrims. The veil of Mary at Chartres Cathedral was reported to have great healing powers. These symbols, through an inflamed imagination, shaped the religious habits and beliefs of the people significantly.

People believed that on the day they went to Mass they were protected from going blind or having a stroke. They also believed they did not grow older during the time spent at Mass. The church encouraged these beliefs as long as dogmatic truth was kept pure and was not confused with pedestrian beliefs. The church fathers were not alarmed by people's tendency to reduce the infinite to the finite, so the mystery of the Divine seemed to disintegrate. Due to the plague, death was ever present, and there was a sense that the end of the world was at hand. People sought comfort from their fears.

Direct experiences with the Divine were contaminated with people's irrational imaginings. Superstition was accepted, and not distinguished from deeper spiritual experience. The church took no responsibility for discernment. They did nothing to help the people distinguish between helpful religious beliefs and distorted imagery. "While offering so much food to the popular imagination," says Huizinga, "the Church could not claim to keep the imagination within the limits of a healthy and vigorous piety." The church overloaded the imagination with symbols and laid the groundwork for reformers who pronounced all imagery destructive.

The only time the pre-Reformation church became defensive was when the mystics talked of annihilation of the personality. They described being absorbed into God that took away the will of the person and rendered him or her incapable of sin. Catherine of Siena said her heart had been changed into the heart of Christ. Others who did not express mystical experiences in such elegant images were burned at the stake.

It was from this suffocating religiosity that people began to run. As the Western world moved into the Enlightenment, we embraced reason as the central function of the mind. This excluded subjective experiences: the senses, as well as intuition, dreams, or any hints of revelation. In the eyes of both scientists and leaders of the Reformation, the religious imagination was stripped of all respect and honor among the various pathways of knowing. The Protestants banished symbols and images from their churches because they thought them idolatrous. The Divine spark that resides in the imagination was all but snuffed out.

After working with the labyrinth for several months, I knew that people's experiences were varied. Many found a deep and peaceful silence within. Yet it seemed that the majority of people received some form of solace or wisdom from a voice. Although people would not identify it as their own, that voice was from within. Saint John of the Cross called this phenomenon "words spoken in the imagination."

Saint John warned us about paying attention to the "words of the imagination" because of the inability of the church to sort out the difference between mysticism and superstition, between genuine religious experience and magical thinking. In keeping with this tradition, Thomas Keating warns us that the "angels and devils cannot perceive what you are doing in contemplative prayer if it is deep enough. They can only know what is in your imagination and memory, and they can add material to these faculties."

Harold Stone put it another way: "For in the imagination is contained all the positive and the highest good; all the negative and the deepest evil." Our fear of the imagination is understandable, but we have abandoned this illuminative field to the devils because we have not taken responsibility for it. We have not learned how to invite the angels in. We have not learned how to utilize its divine connection, its connection to the Source. This is a step we need to take to move on to the transformation that awaits.

However, as the imagination and intuition are coming back into our awareness so too is the reaction to them. The imagination is sustained and encouraged in the open-minded part of the church, and forbidden and censored in another. It is not wise to take our imagination literally. The symbols and images that appear should be opened and reflected upon. As a tool of knowing, the imagination can be quite frightening, especially to people who have used the Bible as their only source of knowing. They try to censor the imagination by banning textbooks that speak of the imaginary worlds, of witches, magic, or of God beyond easy Scriptural understanding.

The new ways of understanding continue to be placed over and against the old ways of understanding our existence on earth. How we know and learn, and how we remain open to the present and future without fear are major challenges in our lives. To those of us who fear our interior world, the ideas behind the labyrinth will shake us to our foundations. However, the experience of the labyrinth, if we let ourselves explore it, could be wondrously supportive and gentle.

We are just beginning to restore the honor of the imagination. And we have yet to sort out the difference between superstition and mystical experience. This lack of distinction can lead to fear and mistrust of enlightening experiences, such as we have in the labyrinth. This may be one of the major reasons that Chartres still denies the public the use of the labyrinth. So our spiritual famine continues. We remain in darkness, unable to see the continuing revelation of the Spirit of God. "Life of the Spirit can only be eternally creative," says the Eastern Orthodox theologian Nicholas Berdyaev. When the church declares that revelation is complete, or even predetermined, then it denies the possibility of the mystery of God. Revelation happens through the human psyche as well as through history, through both the Immanent and the Transcendent God. To deny the imagination is to cut us off from the Holy.

People have revelatory experiences in the labyrinth. At first I was uncomfortable with this. I was concerned that someone might have a distorted experience. After months of walking the labyrinth and listening to the experiences of others, I began to trust the labyrinth. Much more exploration is yet to be done, but seekers frequently meet their spiritual longing, are greeted by a velvety silence, or hear the still, small voice within. They gain wisdom, assurance, solace, peace, and direction. When people take questions into the labyrinth, they receive direct guidance unique to each person's individual context. The following letter is a good example:

I *had been impatient with people lately and it was beginning to affect my work. My hope, once I admitted it to myself, was to get insight about this. I figured if I got any help at all it would be a reminder to stop being impatient, so I entered the labyrinth not expecting to receive much. Frankly I expected a Zen meditation stick reminder on how important patience is. Instead, I received three clear messages, none of which seemed to speak to patience directly. The first was "Spend*

*time with the people you love." The second was
"Make time for creativity" and the third was
"Take time out for retreats."*

*I didn't intellectually understand how this
guidance related to patience. However, the message
seemed crystal clear and it felt right. Later I realized that my impatience was from not taking care
of these parts of myself. I immediately started to
do these things and felt a difference right away. I
still use them for guidelines and have become better
at honoring these sides of myself. It is a discipline
for me to keep them in balance with my busy life.
The labyrinth was a great help in getting me to see
this.*

The reminder that "all revelation is the revelation of
how to search, how to struggle. It is not the revelation of results" gave me clarity and guidance. When
I observed the consistent loving wisdom that people
received from the labyrinth, I began to delve deeper
into sacred geometry in an attempt to discover the
reason behind such pure, clear space. I think it is
because the space is archetypally "perfect," so when
it is dedicated to being sacred, clarity occurs and pu-
rity of heart is released within the heart of the
seeker.

The Demise of the Feminine

The second characteristic of the labyrinth
process is the feminine principle. Respect for

the feminine, like the imagination, is sorely lacking in the Western world today. During the brief period of the High Middle Ages, the courts of love elevated womanhood to great heights. Birth was the central image of the times and the theme for the building of Our Lady of Chartres as well. Unlike other cathedrals, it holds no tombs in the crypt.

The highest of veneration was bestowed upon Saint Mary the Virgin. In fact, according to Favier, the virgin predates Christianity. Even before the birth of Christ, there was at the location of Chartres an altar and a statue to honor the Virgin which medieval texts call *Virgo paritura*. This was the virgin of the Druids, one-third of the Triple Goddess. Some say she was transposed into Mary, the Virgin Mother of Jesus, as the pagans were converted. The monk and mystic Bernard of Clairvaux saw Mary as the incarnation of "original spiritual values." Jean Favier's research tells us that Mary was understood to be the intercessor on behalf of the people directly to her son. People believed that she stood between the earth and heaven, between the natural and the supernatural. She was precious to people because she understood the frailty of the human race. She was a refuge for sinners, and all who approached God did so through her. The Virgin Mary represents the collective images of the feminine aspect of divinity. She was recognized throughout France through the construction of the many Notre Dame Cathedrals that still grace the land.

By the late Middle Ages, the church became embarrassed by the intense devotion to Mary, and worship of her was banned. Consequently, after the fourteenth century there was a lessening of respect for women. Many women lost their property and in some countries became the property of their husbands. The Black Death even contributed to the devaluation of women. The symbol of death during the plague was a "black-cloaked old woman with streaming hair and wild eyes, carrying a broad-bladed murderous scythe. Her feet end in claws instead of toes." During the next three hundred years the fear of death and the growing repression of the imagination and of the natural world fueled one of the deadliest periods of history. The witch burnings are one of the deepest and darkest collective cultural secrets of European history.

Approximately nine million women (and some men) were burned at the stake as witches. Midwives were killed for easing the pain of childbirth. This was seen as usurping the priest's role, and contrary to the biblical injunction that women were to suffer because of Eve. Women who used herbs for healing and had knowledge of nature's way, women who were considered pagan because they observed the seasonal changes and the lunar calendar, were suspect. Women who did not fit into a conventional social role—because they were smart, or unmarried, or childless, or owned property—all lived in fear. Many were being turned in to the authorities, tried unfairly, tortured, and put to death. Most were burned at the stake.

Much was lost. The old religions that embraced the connection to the natural world were destroyed. We lost our connection to creation. We banished the intuitive, pattern-perceiving parts of our selves. The feminine, receptive, holistic way of seeing had been replaced with a blind faith in the truncated rational mind—a mind that understands force and not flow, either/or instead of both/and thinking, competition instead of cooperation, power over instead of power with, short-term thinking instead of planning for the seventh generation.

So, in some strange sense, it is "all about the fourteenth century." For over the ages as we turned our backs on the religious sentiment that defined the God of the Middle Ages, we lost our connection to the invisible world. We turned against the imagination, grew to mistrust symbols, and devalued creativity. Our sense of the whole was lost. Unity is conceptually and experientially beyond the grasp of the human awareness until we unify reason and image. The labyrinth gives us a glimpse of this unity.

Those guided by a vision of wholeness know that the path to discovering God is as varied and unique as each individual seeker. To awaken to the Divine in the context of a culture that is designed to deny is often an uphill battle. Learning to work together and celebrate our differences is hard work. It needs introspection and discernment; it demands action on the individual and collective level. This is the mission of the labyrinth as it reenters our world.

Six

REDISCOVERING THE DIVINE WITHIN

The more faithfully you listen to the voice within you,
the better you will hear what is sounding outside.
And only she who listens can speak.

—*Dag Hammarskjold,* Markings

O ur souls hunger for the lost connection to our intuitive nature expressed through myths, dreams, stories, and images. We long for a creative, symbolic process that nurtures our spiritual nature, that feeds the soul.

We begin to nourish ourselves spiritually when we discover the dimensions of divine/human consciousness, when we begin to discover the Divine within. We need to understand that the spirit of creation lives and evolves within each human being, as well as through the whole of the created order. Many of us sense this mysterious unfolding. And many are seeking experiences that help us respond to the changes this evolution brings into our lives.

We inhabit a planet in danger of dying. Governments around the world are notoriously shortsighted and are dominated by powerful interest groups that do not hold the welfare of society at heart. Other institutions attempt to respond to the needs of the times with bureaucratic rigidity. These old models are no longer effective. This is true of every institution in our society. The family is in the throes of dramatic redefinition. Corporations are beginning to face the fact that they must give back more to society than ever before. They cannot continue to use the world's resources and keep most of the profits. The workplace is being restructured. Education is in desperate need of reorganization and support. Our children are deprived of the rudimentary knowledge they need to be part of the solution to the enormous challenges of the future.

Empirical science has been the major proponent of "If you can't see it and can't measure it, it doesn't exist." This reasoning is beginning to be recognized as part of an evolutionary step we needed to take. But it offers only a limited view, which we have mistaken for the whole picture. The tyranny of the Age of Reason is losing its grip. The human intellect, especially when pushed to its maximum, is limited when not used in harmony with other human faculties. We must look for new models, new definitions, new ways of doing things, even for new human faculties that lie dormant within us. But we don't know how to do this. Without systems in place to keep our societies functioning smoothly, chaotic, misdirected energy is coming to the surface. The labyrinth can serve as a channel for this chaotic energy. It can help us forge new pathways.

Out of this chaos, ideological polarization is occurring. Polarization is based on a process of projection. We carry unchallenged emotional and intellectual conflicts, beliefs, and contradictions within and project them out onto others. We may find ourselves accusing others of the very thing we are doing ourselves.

In this time of growing turmoil, people need an enemy. We need to make people wrong, instead of allowing them to be different. The fear is the same on both sides, but the polarization and explosive rhetoric perpetuate grave misunderstanding. These distortions are kept alive through the media. There is too often no effort at balanced and accurate reporting. This polarized political climate does not allow for sincere discussion. We do not have sufficient tools that encourage people to meet one another on common ground.

A year after the Labyrinth Project was under way, I traveled to Zurich to meet Rosemary Schmid, the woman who organized the Labyrinth Project there. Along with a small group of women, she had secured a community space in which to make a labyrinth. They gathered people together and created a large labyrinth garden that presently has 133 gardeners tending it. The pathways are lined with flowers and vegetables, and children have painted rocks to line the path. After work on summer evenings, people come by to tend the garden, walk the labyrinth, and greet one another in the course of their activity. This project is a wonderful way to bring a community together. Projects such as these are needed to cross-pollinate ideas and break down barriers between people.

In the same spirit, scientists have begun talking to mystics. This is great cause for celebration. This reunion of science and religion can lead us out of the severe divisions of our chaotic times. Only through human contact and mutual sharing of ideas across boundaries can we begin to allow solutions to come into our hearts and minds. We need a vision of unity, we need to realize that we are all on the path together. We need to join together in a communal prayer for ourselves and our planet. One labyrinth walker's anonymous response form echoed this need for community:

> *Thank you for making the labyrinth available! We hear the Episcopal church being characterized for being conservative, closed, stodgy. I am encouraged and proud that we are offering this universal meditation symbol and tool to the entire community.*

The How of Faith

When I was in seminary in the late 1960s, I went through an emotional crisis. I contacted one of the seminary professors trained in pastoral psychotherapy at the Menninger Institute. This was a lifesaving process for me, but the students on campus were divided about utilizing psychotherapy. The open, supportive camp said, "If you need help, go get it." Students from the other camp quietly reminded me that my crisis was simply a lack of faith. If I had more faith, they reasoned, I would not need help. What this second group did not understand is that my faith grew through my reaching out for help. The fact that another human being was willing to sit with me, to guide me as I sorted out my life, was a gift. And what I learned about myself in the process has provided a firm foundation for me to live my life. This was when I realized there was a "how of faith."

What disturbs me about the church is that, Sunday after Sunday, we preach the message of the Gospel: to love one another, to grow in compassion. But we are never able to say how to do this. The church does not address the how of faith, it only points in the direction of the ideal. When we allow the intellect to define our experience of faith, we lose sight of the path. This is why people have sought psychotherapy, from its earliest years to the present, as an avenue of growth. At its best, it offers a healing process that integrates the mind and emotions with the longing of the soul.

But there is a renaissance in Western spirituality, particularly in Christian spirituality. The movement in the church to reclaim its lost spiritual tradition is enormously significant. A trained spiritual director may listen to the seeker and make concrete suggestions about prayer, journaling, or other means of growth. The labyrinth can play a significant role in the field of spiritual direction. It can guide people to glimpses of the Divine. It can help people reach spiritual maturity.

In the past, Christianity has disregarded the need for a spiritual path. It urged people simply to believe intellectually, rather than seek experiences of the Sacred. Systematic theology, originally designed to guide the seeker into a deep understanding of loving God, has mapped out the territory of faith in conceptual terms. Once the faith experience was mapped out, it was mistaken for the actual territory. Consequently, Christianity has retained only part of its content. It has lost sight of the process teachings that guide us along a sequenced, nameable pathway to discover God within ourselves. The labyrinth literally reintroduces the experience of walking a clearly defined path. This reminds us that there is a path, a process that brings us to unity, to the center of our beings. In the simple act of walking, the soul finds solace and peace. This is the point Karen Armstrong made earlier. If we would only tell people that God is not going to be discovered first through the rational mind, it would help them a great deal. This is the importance of the labyrinth. No matter where we are in our own life's journey, no matter what tradition sparks the creative imagination, we may glimpse the Divine. In the following letter, the seeker describes this as being "imprinted by the Spirit":

Walking the labyrinth is a difficult experience to capture in words. Each time I have walked it, I have felt all the peace of a deep meditation and the joy of being involved in and with a community of fellow spiritual beings. I have always come away with something that can be applied immediately to my daily life. It is as if my feet have been imprinted with the spirit. What is most precious to me is that the labyrinth is not attached (necessarily) to a religion but has a wider and more personal spiritual quality. It is not required that one know a certain prayer, have certain parents or be baptized—the only requirement is to put one foot in front of the other.

The Need to Learn Languages of Process and Symbols

The loss of process teaching goes far beyond the modern-day church. It originates in the European languages which "require that verbs or action words be associated with nouns." We can only refer to a process or activity that is connected to a physical thing. This European linguistic trait has hindered our relationship to the invisible world. We have a difficult time talking about a nonmaterial process, such as a growing in faith or forgiveness, or an encounter with the numinous. Cultures with different linguistic structures are able to articulate these processes that were understood to be eternal, as powers, lines, flow of action, or as gods. Many of these cultures that the Western world dismissed as primitive were able to articulate how the energy and creativity of the Spirit became grounded in matter.

This is why stories and symbols are of such prime importance. For example, it is difficult to describe the process of forgiveness because there is no language for it. Some of us think that forgiveness is a simple act of will. But something much deeper has to happen. The following story, "Magic Eyes," is an example of process teaching, focusing on forgiveness.

Fouke was a tall man with a thin chin and nose who worked as a baker. He was known for his righteousness. "He was so upright that he seemed to spray righteousness from his thin lips over everyone who came near him; so the people preferred to stay away." His wife, Helga, was the opposite, round and warm, so people wanted to come close to her to share the "cheer of her open heart." One day Fouke found Helga with another man, and the incident became the talk of the village. Instead of rejecting her, as everyone thought he would, he said that he forgave her. But he only pretended to forgive her "so that he could punish her with his righteous mercy." This did not go well in heaven, so whenever Fouke felt his secret hate, an angel came down and dropped a pebble into his heart. The more Fouke hated his wife, the more pebbles settled into his heart. Over time, it became so heavy that the "top half of his body bent forward so he had to strain his neck to look straight ahead." Finally, the angel came to him and told him how he could be healed of his hurt. He was instructed to ask the angel for Magic Eyes, so that every time he saw Helga he would see a lonely woman who needed him, rather than a wicked woman who betrayed him. Each time he used the Magic Eyes a pebble would be lifted from his heart. Fouke could not do this at first, for he loved his hatred. But eventually the pain in his heart became so great that he asked the angel for the Magic Eyes. Helga began to change before his eyes. His heart grew lighter, he began to stand straight again, he began to laugh and smile. He invited Helga "into his heart again, and she came, and together they began a journey into their second season of humble joy."

This story describes forgiveness in a simple, childlike way. When we hold hatred in our hearts, it keeps us from enjoying life. It spreads until it touches every part of our being. To forgive is to let go of past hurts and to see with new eyes. It can feel like lifting a weight from your heart. There are no words in our language to describe the root of this process. The same is true of talking about the journey of faith, or about developing a love of our enemies. In the labyrinth we can feel the pebbles in our heart. We can experience our holding them in to punish others, which is a part of spiritual immaturity that we all share. The labyrinth is a place where we can let go of the hurt and hard-heartedness.

Most people come out of the labyrinth wanting to maintain a nonverbal state. At workshops, I encourage people to journal or draw mandalas in order to capture in concrete form the inner process that is occurring. Drawing and journaling are process languages. So is working in clay, or any other activity that suspends the linear thought process. Each of us must find a way to this inward part of ourselves. We must have some avenue to connect to our innermost being. For many, the labyrinth can be a way.

Walking the labyrinth immediately takes us into a process world where we can see between the lines of linear thought through to our imagination and intuition. It offers Westerners a nonlinear world which evokes experience that goes beyond the subjective fragments of our own unprocessed history. It moves us beyond the conceptual prison of our thinking mind. It serves as an entryway to the unseen world where we can find, once again, the invisible connection with the great-grandmother's thread.

As I inched closer to the entry place, tears came to my eyes as I watched people, old and young, of different cultures, different histories, walk their paths in their own unique ways, at their own pace. When I finally stepped into it, it felt like going through a birth canal, like being born into my own life. The first half carried with it the excitement and the anticipation of entering the center. As the path wound around, I walked my life, moving very close, then further away from the center over and over again. When I actually stepped into the center I was completely surprised I was there! As I stood in it, I felt as though I had just gathered all the moments of my life, from conception to that very minute. I remembered times I felt very close to my center and times and places that led me further from it. And yet, I was very conscious of the fact that every single moment (person, place, time, thing, event) of my life had brought me to the center right now. Not one iota of it was accidental or unrelated. There is a prayer that a Jewish friend taught me, the Shechehiyanu, that I prayed there: "Thank you, God, for preparing me, for sustaining me, and for bringing me to this moment so that I can truly celebrate what is."

Since our language is limited and we are unable to articulate processes in our linear language, we are experiencing an increase in use of symbolic languages. Systems of symbolic language such as the I Ching, the tarot, runes, and astrology are coming more into our awareness. "To the imagination the sacred is self-evident," Nietzsche reminded us. And it is to the imagination that symbols speak. This is the source of attraction to the labyrinth as well. During the Women's Dream Quest we use the Celtic runes as a way to determine our dream groups. Each leader chooses a rune, then duplicates her rune for the six other people in her group. Themes such as Strength, Joy, Harvest, Wholeness, and Opening set the tenor of the groups. Symbols are rich channels of information when we understand the meaning held within them. Mythologist and author Joseph Campbell once remarked that those who do not know that symbols hold hidden meaning are "like diners going into a restaurant and eating the menu rather than the meal it describes." The soul thinks in symbols. It is not literal-minded. Developing a process language nourishes the soul.

Rediscovering
the Mystical Tradition

A t the core of every religious tradition around the world are mystical traditions that contain teaching stories about direct experiences with the Divine. Vedanta, Sufism, Kabbala, Taoism, Mahayana Buddhism, and Theravada Buddhism are all examples of highly developed systems. "These technologies have in common," writes Andrew Harvey, "the knowledge that the Divine Self is the one essential fact of the cosmos, and ways to reveal and realize it are known and have been charted."

Prayer and meditation are the avenues to direct contact with the Light. They are being restored for use in the Western world. Through prayer we can discover the process that will help us mature as spiritual beings. Many of us are uncomfortable with prayer. We are afraid we will do it wrong, or that our requests will be refused. As we move through the labyrinth, we can move between silence and image. The act of prayer can become playful and joyous.

Prayer is a very powerful avenue to the Divine. The amazing lives of the mystics are examples of this. Julian of Norwich asked God to bring suffering to her so she could understand it. This is a puzzling request, to say the least. But because of her suffering Julian saw the face of Christ in all his compassion. Teresa of Avila exquisitely described the soul as the interior castle each of us possesses. Our lack of exposure to the Christian mystics is understandable, however. They have embarrassed many generations of Christians, clergy and lay people alike. We are frightened of the depth of chaotic experience that can occur when our psyche encounters Spirit. When we contact the Light within, we can become entangled in darkness because our shadow emerges and we are unprepared for its impact. Curiously, for most people who have a profound experience in the labyrinth which involves confrontation, it happens in the most loving way. The person is able over time to integrate it without much conflict. Such is the grace of the labyrinth.

Opening to the sacred is a profound, life-changing process. It frees enormous energy that needs to be channeled back out in the world in service. If the focus is back into the self, then the act of seeking can become an addiction. It can become a self-reinforcing system that does not lead to the spiritual maturity of the seeker.

Many of us assume that the consciousness in which we function during the day is the same consciousness we use in prayer. In our flight to the rational, we have forgotten that there are many subtle layers of consciousness. The act of prayer involves learning to focus our concentration and being open to what we discover in the depths of our being. In the Western world the power of the human will has been given free rein. Prayer became an act of will, which in some traditions led to prayer as a form of self-discipline. This is a severe distortion of the purpose of prayer. It has injured many people who learned to blame themselves when their prayer life was not effective.

The earlier prayer form of *lectio divina* that supported reflection, spontaneous prayer, and contemplation were "reformed" in the fifteenth century. They were replaced by mental prayer and contemplation. Then contemplation was eventually dropped from the tradition because it encouraged direct, mystical experiences. The spiritual path in Christianity has been washed out by the rains of history. Currently attempts are being made to restore contemplation by returning to the *lectio divina*.

Christianity lost its meaning and its power to transform lives when it threw out its mystical teachings. The inner way seemed dangerous and complicated. This is why there has been such an emphasis on the Transcendent God, who is perceived as outside ourselves. Both aspects of God are important, but we have created a religious ideology that values one to the exclusion of the other, and is therefore incomplete. We need the help and guidance of the labyrinth to sort out the many turns and challenges of the spiritual path. The labyrinth is part of the rediscovery of the lost mystical tradition.

Meeting the Immanent God

The Immanent God is the God of the mystics— the still, small voice within. This God is found in Christian Scriptures and is "written in our hearts," but not given much attention. The Holy produces fear and doubt in the minds and hearts of the educated postmodern person. *Sacred* and *scared* are only one letter inversion away from one another. Genuine mystical experiences have been lumped together with superstition and self-absorption. Seekers who have had mystical experiences have been looked upon with suspicion, and often dismissed as flaky. There may be specks of truth in some of these judgments, but they by no means apply to the majority of pilgrims. We can be prone to a shopping mall mentality that encourages us to think that spiritual life is disposable and easy. Those who are especially vulnerable are those who have not embraced any form of the many teaching traditions. However, to make such a negative generalization about how the Spirit is moving in people's lives cuts us off from the very path we need to follow.

The Creator God embraced by the Judeo-Christian tradition is seen as a stern, jealous, male God who acts as easily out of wrath as compassion. Yahweh is a stumbling block for many seekers. The first time I heard Joseph Campbell speak, his thoughts led him to Yahweh, the God of the Old Testament. His face reddened and his voice became strident. Suddenly he burst out with "The trouble with Yahweh is, he thought he was God!" Then, I was surprised that he seemed unable to get beyond his childhood religious upbringing. Years later, this statement looks very different to me. What I then perceived as his inability to move beyond his personal anger, I now understand to be frustrated anger at a system of Western beliefs that limits and distorts the essence of the Holy. It also serves a system that judges those who are different, supports a dis-

torted view of justice, and punishes—without reha-
bilitating—those who break the rules.

Recently, the National Film Board of Canada
sponsored a three-part series on women's spirituality. Luisah Teish, an African American who was
raised Catholic and is now reclaiming her African
spiritual roots, had this to say:

> *The more I listened to what they had to say about
> the great, bearded, white man in the sky, the more
> I realized he was nobody I could talk to. You
> couldn't say nothing to the dude. He didn't an-
> swer prayers, and he could go off on you at any
> minute and you were supposed to be grateful no
> matter what he did. This is nobody who made any
> kind of sense to me so, in my naïveté, I put him
> down and hung with Mary.*

Biblical scholars and theologians tell us this is
not necessarily an accurate interpretation of the Old
Testament God embraced by Christianity. I happen
to believe it is not. But what they believe or what I
believe makes very little difference when most people
believe in a punitive God. This stern, jealous male
God is repugnant to many people. This Yahweh is
supposed to have been the God that created all of
the natural order, usurping the role of the Mother,
the creator of life. Yahweh, God the Father, is the
only version of the Transcendent God that is offered
in Western Christianity. He is seen as the first cause
of all things, the God of history. He is a faraway
God whom we do not know personally. He does not

seem to want to know us either. This jealous God says, "You shall have no graven images before me." This merciless God is being reconstituted as a present-day model for judgment and punishment against anyone who is different. The church does not seem aware that God the Father blocks the way of people attempting to relate to the Christian path. It doesn't help that the church refuses to deal with this struggle. It is rather ironic that the Jewish tradition does not hold Yahweh as rigidly as the Christians do.

Even more difficult is the "theology of the elect" that arises from time to time in monotheistic religions. Fundamentalism is enlivened by the concept of the theology of the elect that is "clearly shown in the holy wars that have scarred the history of monotheism," says Karen Armstrong. She goes on to say, "Instead of making God a symbol to challenge our prejudice and force us to contemplate our own shortcomings, it can be used to endorse our egotistic hatred and make it absolute. It makes God behave exactly like us, as though he were simply another human being." But in our predominantly Christian, Western civilization, we still think this God is safer than the one we sense we may find inside ourselves.

In *Woman as Healer,* Jeanne Achterberg makes the historical observation that during difficult and chaotic times we embrace a more brutal God. This is true today amid the chaos and fear generated as we cross into the twenty-first century. Women are more suppressed and healers are censored. The distorted Transcendent God never changes. He is omnipresent, jealous of other deities, and remains firmly in place. No wonder some seekers have remained aimless sojourners. "When God is only object over and against subject," says James Nelson, "immanence recedes and when immanence fades even God's transcendence becomes less real." This is the prism through which we understand the Divine, and it is severely out of balance. The God within exists where image meets silence. This is the way of the Immanent God.

A woman was struggling with these very concerns. She chose to live her life according to the Benedictine rule and was struggling with what obedience to Christ meant. She walked into the labyrinth at the end of the week-long conference and asked, "What do I need to leave behind?" She heard, "Obedience to the rules." Then she asked, "What do I need to take with me?" She heard, "Learn to follow Christ." The woman was puzzled. What was the difference? She heard, "Obedience to the rules is mindless; following Christ is mindful." The woman left the conference jubilant. A question central to her life had been answered.

Reclaiming the Body

Many of us—men and women alike—struggle with our relationship to the physical body. Yet it is the foundation from which we build the rest of personhood. Often we do not experience an awareness of our bodies until we attempt to express intimate and sexual feelings. But when we open ourselves to experiencing the constrictions and the flexibility of our bodies, we also open ourselves to the joy of living in our bodies.

We often repress feelings of contempt for our bodies if we feel deficient in any way. The tragedy of incest or abuse may have cut us off from the experience of our body as a base. We may carry a birthmark we are disgusted with, may have experienced a childhood disease that left us physically challenged, or discovered we were gay and did not know what to do with feelings that are never safe to talk about.

Walking the labyrinth is a body prayer. It is nonthreatening; all we are asked to do is to walk. Even those of us with the deepest inner divisions can do that. Moving through the labyrinth, we can learn what it feels like to stand firm in the world. We sense our feet firmly planted on the ground, our legs, pelvis, torso, arms, neck, and head flowing with energy and life.

When we are grounded in our bodies, we are stabilized and can receive information more accurately. Much like fine-tuning a radio, if we are attuned to our bodies the static in the incoming messages and impulses is reduced. To reclaim the body is a sacred act. In doing so, we may discover a path to the Divine. Dancing, skipping, crawling, or solemnly walking are all encouraged on the labyrinth. The more free and spontaneous we are in the labyrinth, the more energy we bring into our lives.

Transforming the Shadow

Unfortunately, some of the new spiritualities deny the shadow side of life. Pain and suffering are seen as a creation of our own minds that many erroneously believe we need to suffer. Half truths are taken as whole truths and the mystery of pain and human darkness that sometimes shapes and motivates us is overlooked. Taking responsibility for ourselves easily gets confused with blaming ourselves. Jung said, "One does not become enlightened by imagining figures of light, but by making the darkness conscious." This is how the shadow is transformed. The shadow has to come to light. Getting to know our shadow is the most important spiritual work we can do at this time.

In the Christian tradition the focus of self-knowledge is on the discovery of the shadow. If it continues to be denied it will be projected outward onto others. This is what we see happening in the propagation of hate and tribalism. The individually disowned shadow is the engine behind collective racial hatred, homophobia, and religious wars. As righteous aggressors we cannot see the hypocrisy of our actions. We kill in the name of God. The person who knows himself knows the difference between the light and shadow, the personal and universal. He knows that the imagination can serve in the purpose of the Light. Intention is key. We can guide ourselves through difficult periods of personal upheaval, when anger arises and we seek revenge. Part of any spiritual practice is to work with the shadow.

Since the shadow is unconscious by definition, it

may take the loving kindness of others to direct our attention to it. It may also become apparent when things go wrong in life. We may find ourselves sitting on a crate in a strange apartment we were forced to rent when our spouse ordered us out of the house. We may feel wronged. We may have no idea that our outbursts or rage, our incessant criticism were part of the dance that led us to this crate. When we are in the grips of the shadow, we don't realize how we hurt others. It must come to our attention and we must have the skill to deal with it, or to seek help in transforming it. We cannot be loving to others if we are filled with anger and hurt. It is our responsibility to work out those feelings. To focus on this while walking the labyrinth can be healing. A personal shadow exists within each of us. To recognize that peeling away its layers is a lifelong task is a measure of spiritual maturity. This is what comes into focus on the labyrinth. We can see our fears clearly. We can begin to sense where we are being unfair to others. We can begin to sense the great-grandmother's thread.

Connecting the Inner World with the Outer

The Western world has lived under the assumption that the outer world is objective and the inner world is subjective. By this definition, objective means reliable, concrete, and meaningful, while subjective means unreliable, hollow, and useless as a pathway of knowing. The scientific myth, helped along by Freud, has taught us to trust the outer world. However, as the empirical method breaks down and science broadens its borders, this is up for redefinition. There is an objective inner world and a subjective outer world within each of us. The Immanent God is found in our inner, objective experience. To discover the voice of the inner world is to discover the voice of the soul. Laurens van der Post makes the point that it is through the "sensibilities of the imagination" that we perceive this inner, objective place. When the imagination travels through the psyche, archetypal symbols release energy which creates meaning that is experienced as sacred. This is what Nietzsche meant when he said that to the imagination the sacred is self-evident. This is especially apparent when people approach the labyrinth for the first time. Frequently their response is awe.

We are in danger today of being engulfed by the collective shadow once again. The Cold War was the symbolic dam that kept the waters of change in check. Now the dam has broken, and the waters are choked with hatred and fear—but also with new seeds of spiritual revolution. We are entering a time of ever-increasing chaos and the impulse is to repress the imagination, when it is the very thing we need in order to discover the Immanent God.

The Apocalyptic myth of the end of time is fuel for the fire of the collective shadow. In theory, only the select people will survive—only those who have followed the rules. This belief is gaining momentum in a world where fear has filled our imaginations. As Christians we are taught to abide in love for all living things and to stand in judgment over no one.

This is a far cry from what is happening in the world. We are afraid to envision a peaceful world; we are afraid to accept one another. Western civilization is blocked at this juncture. We lack the vision and the skills to move ahead to the next stage of spiritual evolution.

Gandhi was once asked, "What do you think of Western Civilization?" He replied, "I think it would be a good idea." Part of our collective shadow is our belief that we are superior. We have asserted our superiority many times: over Native Americans, over African slaves. We have elaborate mechanisms of denial that keep us from seeing ourselves. We must claim our collective shadow in order to continue any semblance of a civilization into the twenty-first century. The labyrinth can be a boat in these swirling waters of change.

THE LABYRINTH: BLUEPRINT FOR TRANSFORMATION

*It may be time, psychologically speaking, for us to
ground our vision in the principle of the feminine
archetype . . . The gaze of theoretical-instrumental reason needs to be reintegrated with a vision of wholeness,
a vision of feeling, a vision of life.*

—*David Michael Levin,* The Opening of Vision

Recently, I talked with friends about whether
tool is the best word to describe the labyrinth. I
went to the thesaurus and looked up *gadget, device,
mechanism,* and *apparatus.* None of the words better
expressed what I want to say than *tool.* But what
kind of tool? In essence, the winding path of the
labyrinth offers a blueprint for the psyche to meet
the soul.

One Saturday in Lent my friend Barbara and I took the labyrinth to a local church for a workshop. After my presentation, we began to guide participants into the labyrinth. The second person to begin was an elderly woman with a cane who was very hard of hearing. It became apparent to me that the pattern confused her, because she missed the first turn. By the next turn I stepped in and offered her my arm, which she willingly took. I knew that I could not talk with her easily or quietly, so I chose silence as I began to lead her around the winding path. She took to it easily then, not placing her weight on my arm, but simply using it to balance herself. We settled in with each other, finding a pace that was comfortable. I looked around somewhat self-consciously at first, and then realized that I was doing what I needed to do. It was the first time I had walked the labyrinth like this—an old woman on my arm . . .

Suddenly memories of my grandmother flooded into my mind. We had often walked just like this. Not long before her death at eighty-six, she was out on the swing in the backyard enjoying the summer breeze by the river. The unruly neighbor kids came over to play. Gram saw them coming and moved, with great difficulty, as quickly as she could into the house. She said that she was not going to be used by the kids, she wasn't a baby-sitter. I was surprised at this. She had always been there for me, so I couldn't imagine she was not going to be available for them. It was one of the first memories I have of her setting conscious boundaries and deciding where and with whom she wanted to spend her time. I was in college at the time.

As the labyrinth walk continued, my mind floated to another long-forgotten memory. I thought with guilt of an old woman I met during my time as a social worker in Philadelphia. Her case was assigned to me, so I went to her home to see her. She was dehydrated, could not feed herself, had no family to help, and needed hospitalization. I reported it and made the arrangements. She was moved to the hospital that afternoon, leaving her frail sixteen-year-old tabby cat with no one to feed her. I took the cat to my home, which I shared with five other people. I waited for several weeks until it was clear that the woman was not going to return home, then had the cat put to sleep. The woman had been wholly unprepared for illness, let alone death. She was very angry at me for hospitalizing her in the first place. She kept telling me that no one can understand another until she walks a mile in that person's shoes. She was not a generous spirit, was straining with nastiness under the trauma of her life, and was unable to forgive.

So there I was on the labyrinth, guiding an old woman around on my arm, overflowing with past experiences of elderly women. I questioned my own ability, even at forty-eight, to extend myself graciously when push comes to shove. I know that place in myself that my grandmother showed me when she ran and hid from the neighbor's kids. She was always generous and loving to my brother and sister and me, but I am sure she felt her powers waning. She died that August, not two months later.

I could be unrelentingly angry if I were an elderly woman and lost my beloved cat and my home.

That day the labyrinth provided an opportunity to reflect on my own as well as others' generous and uncharitable hearts. I felt surrounded by the great-grandmother's thread connecting me to insights and teachings I needed for the challenges staring me in the face, but had not known it until that day.

The Labyrinth Is an Archetype

Archetypal images," Jung says, "decide the fate of man." Jung placed archetypes at the center of his psychological theory, and brought them to our attention. He defined an archetype as "a figure—be it a daimon, a human being, or a process—that constantly recurs in the course of history and appears wherever creative fantasy is freely expressed." These forms exist independently of the human psyche in the collective unconscious and are governed by their own laws. They include figures—spirals, trees—and geometric designs—circles, squares, triangles. The collective unconscious is the invisible realm of symbols and forms that are free-floating throughout our world. The forms in the collective unconscious are universal. They can be found in art and religious symbology all over the world. The labyrinth is simply one example of an archetype.

The collective unconscious is different from the personal unconscious because the symbols and forms that appear in much of our dream life are not necessarily universal. Our dreams can tap into the collective unconscious in what Jung calls a "big dream." Usually when this happens we sense that the dream has some spiritual meaning within it.

There are hundreds, perhaps thousands, of archetypes in use again during these spiritually fervent times; the Great Mother, the Wise Old Man, various female gods from Greek mythology (Artemis, Athena, Hestia), and the triune aspects of the Goddess: the Mother, the Maiden, and the Crone.

There are many Christian archetypes: the cross, the flickering light of a candle, the Divine Child, the Book, the fish symbol called Pisces, the Trinity, the Mother, and the Virgin. All point to the sacred beyond the symbol and open the terrain of the psyche that responds to the numinous. Jung identified Christ as "the perfect symbol of the hidden immortal within the mortal man." It is this hidden immortal, with whom we connect in our unconscious minds, that either initiates or fulfills our search for the Holy. Because each of us has a unique set of human experiences, the same symbols touch each of us differently. The empty cross can mean suffering and sacrifice to one person. To another it can mean liberation and victory over death.

The labyrinth is unusual because it is an archetype with which we can have direct experience in the outer world. We can literally walk it. Usually archetypes are psychological processes that other people cannot see or experience along with us. Archetypes are part of the hard wiring of the collective unconscious.

The archetype that is enlivened in the labyrinth is the archetype of transformation. The circle, which expresses wholeness and unity, is the central archetype, which Jung called the Self. When people walk the labyrinth, many sense that it is a form of communal prayer. The connection between inner and outer becomes the great-grandmother's thread, and we see that we are all connected through the thread to form the web of creation.

Archetypes stand in their own evolutionary time and exist to help the transformation and maturation of human consciousness. They arise and disappear again like great whales breaking the surface of the ocean. Archetypes are like the jewels scattered forth from Her hand to give us clues and vehicles for opening ourselves to the greater mysteries of life. When we contact an archetype, it is like releasing a time capsule in the psyche. We contact the power of the numinous. Jung described it "as though chords in us were struck that had never resounded before, or as though forces whose existence we never suspected were unloosed." The breath of life is breathed back into us, and we are spurred on to live life more fully.

Jung also described archetypes this way: "Archetypes are like riverbeds which dry up when the water deserts them, but which it can find again at any time. An archetype is like an old watercourse along which the water of life has flowed for centuries digging a deep channel in itself. The longer it has flowed in this channel the more likely it is that sooner or later the water will return to its old bed."

Many of us are seeking ways to integrate our psychology with our spirituality, our psyche with our spirit. This cannot be achieved without responding to the archetypal symbols that meet us as we live our lives. We sense that metaphor and symbol are a pathway to discovering, really rediscovering, ancient archetypes that hold the keys to transformation. The labyrinth is indeed an ancient archetype, a sleeping giant that is stirring during this time of suffering and uncertainty. It is an old watercourse that is glistening with fresh, clear waters that invite us to drink.

The Labyrinth as a Container

Organically, we know that the right hemisphere and the left hemisphere of the brain function differently and respond to different types of data. If the left brain is more analytical, the right is more intuitive. We also know that the corpus callosum at the center of the brain is the place where the brain's electrical impulses meet. It produces images that allow us to function in the everyday world. Though a great deal of our world demands rational thought, behind rationality many of us find a system of images that informs our experience.

One of the tasks of a therapist is to help the client develop an ego to function in the world. However, it is better to build our ego *around* something, rather than *for* something. In order to have flow between the inner and outer worlds, we need to have a container in which it can take place. Usually, a space is created in the psyche. This intrapsychic space begins to develop through mirroring activities between infants and parents and ends with the psychological differentiation between parent and child. It is in this space that the imagination sparks. In my mind's eye, it's like an electrical spark that jumps from one side of the brain to the other. A healthy, balanced person enjoys spending time alone as well as having time with spouse and friends. The ability to sustain our own inner world is invaluable. It ensures that we don't collapse into fear or despair when we are on our own: we know how to nurture ourselves with a good book, a good meal, or a walk along the beach.

Being comfortable with ourselves is only part of it. A sense of spaciousness allows us to respond rather than react in our lives. Within this space we hold the ability to see through the distortions of our minds. This spaciousness can be destroyed early on by manipulative parenting. It can be distorted by a parent's projections: a mother who is continually trying to fix her beautiful daughter's appearance, a father who tells his son he will never make it in the world. As loving as these people may have attempted to be, they were unable to be receptive to objective experience. They were driven by their own unresolved concerns.

Joseph Campbell underscored our need to create this space within:

You must have a room or a certain hour of the day or so, where you do not know who your friends are, you don't know what you owe anybody or what they owe you—but a place where you can simply experience and bring forth what you are and what you might be . . . At first, you may find nothing's happening . . . but if you have a sacred

place and use it, take advantage of it, something
will happen.

He is talking about a room of our own that allows us
to experience our inner world. The room is a space
that provides safety, where the inner and outer can
meet and become one. This is where meaning is produced. We find the great-grandmother's thread when
the inner and outer worlds flow together. When our
worlds are connected through open, receptive consciousness, meaning begins to flow into our lives.
This connection between the inner and outer worlds
is completed through the human faculty of the
imagination.

The Concept of Sacred Space

Sacred space is by definition the place where two
worlds flow into each other, the visible with the
invisible. The finite world touches the infinite. In
sacred space we can let down our guard and remember who we are. The rational mind may be released.
In sacred space we walk from chronos time to kairos
time, as we allow our intuitive self to emerge. "If the
doors of perception were cleansed," said William
Blake, "everything would appear to humans as it
really is: infinite."

Sacred space is traditionally associated with
churches. When I walk into the French Gothic architecture of Grace Cathedral, the soul does seem to
breathe easier. But sacred space can be anywhere, is
everywhere, especially when we are able to remain in

an open, receptive consciousness. Friends told me about making a labyrinth in the sand at the beach north of San Francisco. They played in it with their children and walked it ritually. As they left that day, they saw cloud formations that appeared to them as a great bird they felt blessing them on their way. This is sacred play.

The labyrinth walk offers support for the space inside ourselves so we can see through our distortions. We recognize our impatience, we see the repetition of our judgments about people. One person who was struggling to free himself of anger walked the labyrinth. He found that the image of a person with whom he was not reconciled kept appearing on his shoulder. He realized that he was holding a grudge, a chip on his shoulder if you will. He knew he needed to release the role of victim. In the labyrinth, the feeling of being surrounded by love gives us the support we need to look within.

The possibility of the labyrinth serving as a blueprint for transformation is as startling as it is exciting. When psyche and soul are reunited, so too are the imagination and the thinking mind. The characteristics of the images that people receive during the receptive visualization are the same as those of images received by creative people in a moment of illumination. "These characteristics include the following: a feeling of correctness, a feeling of surprise, a sense of the answer appearing whole, a sense of the answer appearing in shorthand form; one image or word expressing a complicated concept, a sense of the answer appearing in symbolic form, and a feeling of release and joy if the image relates to an important problem."

If we can unify these faculties, we may be on the verge of developing new human capacities, or at least restoring ancient ones. If we can discover new potential within us, we can approach our social problems in new ways. We could gain new skills to create workable communities. We are quickly learning to maneuver in cybernetic space. If we could learn to navigate our inner space as well, new ways of knowing and new ways of communicating would develop.

The Feminine Principle

When we walk into the path of the labyrinth, a new world greets us. This world is not riddled with splits and divisions between mind and body. Woven within this experience is a new vision of reality, an evolutionary step that many people do not yet grasp. But it is before us nonetheless. The key to unlocking the power of this new vision lies in understanding what is meant by the feminine principle, and how to integrate it with the masculine. Through honoring the feminine we may achieve stability, the wisdom and capacity to respect feelings and thoughts, the power to internalize in the body as well as transcend with the mind. We must integrate the faculties of the mind with the images of the soul. This letter came from a participant in the conference on Ancient Spiritual Paths:

I *walked the labyrinth nine times. It was different each time. I enjoyed finding a way to adapt my*

rhythm to the music that was offered. With the
chanting, I found myself walking until a pause in
the liturgy, then resuming walking as they chanted
another phrase. In the "new age" music I found
an easy rhythm to follow, an inner dancing in the
outward form of walking. Sometimes I lost balance
and stumbled and caught myself. Sometimes I
flowed along the path. I found the diversity of ex-
perience on the labyrinth a mirror of life. Some-
times we are independent and individuating,
sometimes we are in community. It became
poignantly clear that we are all in this journey to-
gether.

The values of the feminine principle are beginning to emerge. We need to nurture whole vision,
empathy, patience, organic unfolding and movement, intuition, community, and reverence for nature. This is where the labyrinth shines forth, for
when we walk into this nonlinear path we experience
another way of seeing things.

When we see the whole from this perspective we
experience God-in-process. We understand that we
are part of the divine order. The revelation of the
Divine is unfolding through us—not simply as truth
from on high, but in physical form, in conjunction
with all other forms of life. Seeing and creating
from this whole perspective is the foundation of the
new paradigm that we must embrace to survive in
the twenty-first century.

The letter above gives us a sense of what it is like
to be comfortable with this new world. The labyrinth

can make that easier for most of us if we surrender to the experience: allowing, not forcing, receiving not shaping, accepting not judging. We must be like the martial artist whose power comes not from making things happen but from surrendering to what occurs and then responding from a centered place.

Rhythm is the first aspect of the feminine principle that needs to be honored. When we are in the rhythm with ourselves we can join in harmony with others. This idea first came to my awareness several years ago. I went with friends to a *Messiah* singalong. Thousands of us packed ourselves into the symphony hall for a wonderful evening of singing. At the end, we had to exit all at once. Under ordinary circumstances it would have been a trying experience of stopping and starting, moving a few inches, and being jostled by others. But this evening our hearts were uplifted. The crowd began to sing Christmas carols, and flowed like molten lava out of the auditorium and down the stairs into the street. The harmony of the music created a harmonious feeling among us, and the true joy of Christmas was shared among us.

A sense of community forms within us during the labyrinth walk. But before we can feel connected to one another in community, we must discover our own rhythm. Rarely do we set our own pace, rarely do we know our natural rhythms. One of the first things we notice when entering the labyrinth is that our bodies signal what speed they want to go. Most people slow down during the first part. Honoring our body's tempo helps open our intuitive channels. The creative process joins the imagery moving beneath the surface of our everyday minds to the thoughtful parts of our rational mind. Entering the pulse of our natural flow is the key.

The discovery of our own rhythm begins to lead us to the Sacred. We become aware that we are all part of the dance, that everything around us is part of a divine plan. When we allow the part of ourselves that discerns pattern to come into focus, we receive the outer world differently. Through a soft-eyed approach we see our everyday experiences as part of a bigger pattern. The task is to step beyond the ego, beyond our habit of observing without participating, beyond our habit of judging from the limits of our intellect.

> . . . the labyrinth became a place of gratitude for each other—the handclasp, the pausing for embrace, the deep homesickness for others with whom we would soon be parted. Silent embrace—what volumes it speaks. Another day, a day when I was annoyed with myself for not "getting my time" at the one-thirty dream session, I found the dream unraveling itself unbidden. When I came off the labyrinth, streams of rain were blanketing the doorways. The grace of God was pouring down.

Discovering our connection to the sacred whole empowers our seeking. When we see our lives from the perspective of wholeness, we appreciate that our actions have a greater impact on the world than we may have imagined.

The re-emergence of the feminine principle in

the Western world is not without pain and struggle. The damage done both by the church and by our culture is slow to repair. One woman who came to my workshop was deeply wounded by her Roman Catholic education. She had internalized the principle of unworthiness before she developed any sense of self-esteem. She still felt the effects of this experience but had the inner strength to bring her anger to the workshop. During a walk when I used a Gregorian chant, the woman was so vividly reminded of her religious upbringing that she was unable to enter the room when it was playing. Other people have also reacted against traditional church music because of the unacknowledged damage the church has done.

David Howie, a Bay Area dowser, described the labyrinth as "the skeleton of the Holy Spirit." The phrase has stayed with me. The act of walking the labyrinth can be the act of acknowledging that the powers of good surround our sacred longing. Then we are opening, inviting the flow of the Holy Spirit into our lives. The more I work with the labyrinth, the more deeply I feel that this is the core of its power and allure.

The church is struggling with the issue of whether to address the Holy Spirit in the masculine or feminine. In my mind there is no doubt that the Holy Spirit captures the essence of the feminine side of God. It is the cosmic oneness, the receptive part of the Godhead that allows and understands the flow of our lives. It is the essence of God that helps us see our mistakes clearly, and transform them into building blocks for the next step in our lives. She protects and guides, is patient and merciful. This is the medieval understanding of Mary: the Mother of Jesus, Theotokos, the Mother of God, as embraced by the Eastern Christian Church.

Another understanding of the Mother emerges from the Eastern teachings of the Hindus, Sufis, and Buddhists:

> In the Eastern understanding the spider is the symbol of the Mother. My Mother is both within and without this phenomenal world . . . Giving birth to the world, she lives within it. She is the Spider and the world is the spider's web she has woven . . . The spider brings the web out of herself and then lives in it.

The Mother God weaves the web of creation; it is all-encompassing in its twists and turns, reflecting the presence of the Divine. Maharishna reminded us, "Enlightenment is always knowing the mother is at home."

In the symbology of the labyrinth, Adriadne's thread is the guiding force that leads Theseus to safety. The labyrinth holds the powerful imagery of Mary, the Mother of God. Saint Augustine called Mary the living mold of God. Bernard of Clairvaux wrote of Mary:

> When you follow Her you cannot take a wrong turning; when you pray to Her, you cannot lose

hope; when she fills your thoughts, you are shel-
tered from all error; when she holds you up, you
cannot fall: When she protects you, you are never
afraid; when she leads you forward, you are never
tired; when her grace shines on you, you arrive at
your goal . . .

This merciful, gentle God is the God people are seeking. Some find mercy in Christ, whose teachings illustrate his wisdom and compassion: "Blessed are the poor in spirit, for theirs is the kingdom of heaven. Blessed are the meek, for they will inherit the earth. Blessed are the merciful, for they will receive mercy. Blessed are the pure in heart, for they will see God. Blessed are the peacemakers, for they will be called children of God." But for many people outside the church, Jesus as the Christ is another association with the patriarchy.

Many people think that the feminine understanding of God is a milk-toast version of religion. But many more are grasping for a new understanding of the Holy. The state of the human race is so desperate, so desolate, so dark, that we long for a merciful and gracious God who will empower us to forgive ourselves and one another. It is going to take a soul-filled God for many people to find peace within.

Discernment

I want to share two different images of spiritual discernment with you. The first is the story of a friend who decided to take up white-water canoeing. He joined a group of enthusiasts and took lessons to master the basics. Then he canoed on waters that were rated to match his skills. Periodically he took skill tests to measure his progress in mastering the untamed waters and to receive certification for a new level of difficulty. If only the spiritual life lent itself to the same clarity of progress. The inner life requires an awareness and capacity for reflection that cannot easily be measured or simply tested in safe waters—let alone the unpredictable rapids along the river to the Divine.

In *Dialogue with a Modern Mystic* Andrew Harvey and Mark Matousek discuss the benefits of a spiritual discipline. Harvey refers us to Rumi, the twelfth-century Persian mystic who said that the true seeker needs to become a "pharmacist of bliss." Harvey continues: "You must learn how to play yourself, just as a sitarist knows exactly how to play his or her instrument. There are times when you need to focus, to fast, to retreat, and others when you need to play. The seeker has to know, like a doctor, what remedy is most effective for every nuance of illness. Imagine that in the pharmacy there are five hundred different vials, one is marked 'Aretha Franklin,' another marked 'meditation,' another 'talking long-distance with one's best friend' . . . At any moment, the practiced seeker will know exactly which vial to mix with which. You become the inner inventor of your own joy. The whole of your life becomes a way of helping yourself by innumerable means to enter your deep Self."

But how does one find enough peace within to learn the wisdom of the inner pharmacist who knows how to choose the right vial, the sitarist who knows how to pluck the right string? There is a long way between these two understandings of discernment. When people have plummeted to their spiritual depths, a source of guidance is often needed—a spiritual director, a pastor, a therapist. We cannot travel the journey of Spirit alone. Only people who have mastered the white water of the Spirit can become their own pharmacist of bliss. But that is the ideal for all of us.

Discernment is an important element of the labyrinth experience that cannot be overlooked. Literally thousands of people have walked the labyrinth, in psychically and spiritually challenging environments such as all-night cathedral events. No negative psychological or spiritual upheaval has occurred. The labyrinth has worked only to deepen the insight of the people under stress. The labyrinth is safe territory for many who feel they are unraveling at the seams; it is a place to order chaos and calm the frightened heart.

A therapist came to the labyrinth one night because one of her clients had walked the labyrinth and found great stability and clarity. He had been suicidal and refused medication. As he walked, he experienced a breakthrough that led him off the shaky ground of thinking about taking his own life. In the next session, the client told her of his experience. She wanted to experience the labyrinth for herself. And she wanted me to know about her client. The boundaries of the labyrinth set limits. The structure of the path provides safety for a person who longs to touch deep inside himself.

Like the symbols in dreams, I would not encourage anyone to take the symbols they receive on the labyrinth literally. That is rarely the intention of the subconscious. One woman walked the labyrinth and felt she had been told to sell everything she owned. Ironically, she had just spent the week packing all her belongings and putting them in storage for an extended trip to the East Coast. I spoke with her recently, three years after her labyrinth experience. The message she received had challenged her, but she now looks back on it as an intuitive understanding that she was going to relocate permanently in the East. Her belongings are still in storage, and it is going to be inconvenient to return to dispose of them.

If you feel that you have received a literal message, I would advise you to talk it over with a friend or counselor. And just as in other circumstances, someone who is under the impression that he or she has been selected to carry out a mission that hinders or hurts others is being controlled by a distorted ego. Any action you take should be guided by the insight that we are all spiritual beings, working our way toward wholeness and the mystery behind our calling. When we are in doubt about how to work with our inner life, we should reach out for help. This is true for all spiritual experiences, not just the ones you may have in the labyrinth.

One of the most important areas of discernment

is the ability to distinguish a true experience of the Divine. Magical thinking is one of the biggest pitfalls of spiritual development. Sorting out how the Divine works in our lives is an important spiritual task. If we perceive God as a rescuing God, then we may be naive in our beliefs and the way we function in the world. One woman came to walk the labyrinth at the Mansion House in Dublin, Ireland. The labyrinth was open to the public, so we had no control over pickpockets. We could only warn people to keep their valuables with them. This woman felt invulnerable. She felt it was her special time to walk the labyrinth. But when she returned to her coat, her entire week's salary had been stolen. She was dismayed. As she talked with the sponsor of the workshop, she realized that she had felt protected when she wasn't at all. She was caught up in her newfound spiritual flow, in a habit of magical thinking. The woman assumed that God would take care of her earthly concerns, including her safety and finances. In the end, she was grateful that a week's salary was all she had lost.

As we mentioned earlier, all revelation is about struggle and insight into the process of the unfolding Spirit. It is not about results. Only the Spirit of God, working in our lives, produces results. Jesus said: "By their fruits you shall know them." The gift of life is given to everyone. We all belong to God; this realization sets the movement of the Spirit in motion. When our gifts are grounded in the physical plane, they take root and flourish—through books, music, or art. The gifts of others take root and contribute to our families or communities.

I remain concerned that our spiritual hunger is so great that any shred of the numinous could be overvalued—leading to inflation—or undervalued—leading to a "been there, done that" attitude. A woman in her early twenties came to a workshop and walked the labyrinth three times. On her second walk, she got in touch with profound feelings of anger and grief over her spiritual upbringing. Instead of writing about her feelings, she had a strong need to move away from them. She walked the labyrinth again, but she left dissatisfied with her experience. It is not only the young and inexperienced who are prone to this. Many of us rifle through our experiences without reflection. To people like this, the labyrinth could become a fad, just another thing to do, to try without reflecting deeply on the experience.

The modern church has reason to sound a note of caution during these times of chaos. We need spiritual disciplines to channel the insight and energy that can overwhelm the human psyche whether it is centering prayer, walking the labyrinth, painting a picture, or writing in your journal. The mind needs release from itself in order to find peace, and wisdom. The inner world needs to flow into the outer and back again so we remember the invisible thread that weaves all of existence together.

Both our fear of and our attraction to the Sacred can lead us into an unfocused and reactive spiritual path. We may resist settling down into one practice. Sampling many approaches is not a bad way to begin our spiritual search, particularly if we are trying to break away from one specific tradition or coming out of a cult experience. Explore as many traditions and teachers as possible. But remember that we should be able to find a method or a path that helps stabilize and focus our search. The labyrinth can be a place of refuge for someone who is overwhelmed and seeking.

Ritual and the Labyrinth

An exciting element of spiritual transformation that is beginning to grow is the use of ritual within small groups. Until the last ten or fifteen years, ritual was the territory of organized religion. It fell under suspicion during the rebellious sixties. The word *ritual* became negatively associated with habit, repetition, and therefore boredom. Now, large and small groups, traditional and nontraditional, are discovering the power of simple rituals. When thoughtfully done, they create cohesion, introduce symbols and stories, and lead the individuals to dis-cover the Sacred.

Ritual can be used to mark milestones in life's process. It can honor rites of passage such as the birth of a child, the passage from childhood into adolescence, or the creation of an extended family. It can also be used creatively to share gratitude for the long life of a person with HIV, express support for victims of crime, or honor a woman as she moves through menopause into the age of wisdom. Ritual fulfills our need to honor, acknowledge, and empower as we move through life's transitions. It is a vehicle to heal ourselves, our social fabric, and our planetary home. Unfortunately, the rediscovery of ritual is taking place primarily outside the church.

When we first offered the labyrinth to the public, I usually gave a short overview of its history and presented suggestions about how to use it as a modern spiritual tool. Then we guided people into the labyrinth, allowing a minute before we invited the next person to begin the walk. As the work developed, I began offering workshops in parishes, seminaries, and various psychological and spiritual conferences. Work with the labyrinth became more focused, and ritual around and on the labyrinth became an important refinement. Labyrinth ritual can be very subtle and should never be imposed. Most of what I suggest here captures what feels instinctively natural to the act of walking the labyrinth.

A Bowing Ritual I always invite people to pause before entering the labyrinth. This allows people to catch up with themselves emotionally and to prepare for the walk inwardly. It also emphasizes the decisive first step into the labyrinth.

At the end of the walk, it seems natural to turn around and honor the meditation with a slight bow of the head or whatever other action captures the essence of the moment for you. It is important to respect this impulse if it arises. If you have given yourself permission to follow your impulses throughout the walk, you are less likely to feel self-conscious at the end.

Warming the Labyrinth Each time I open the labyrinth in the cathedral or at a workshop, I gather the handful of people who have made the day possible and invite them to walk directly into the center with me. Standing in a circle, holding hands, we ask that the labyrinth become sacred space and we invoke the Holy Spirit to be present in the labyrinth. We express our hopes, out loud or silently, for the people walking the labyrinth. We ask that they find healing and self-knowledge. This brief ritual brings everyone to the sacred time and acknowledges those whose efforts have made the experience of the labyrinth available to others.

The art is to develop a ritual process around a theme that arises out of the circumstances that have brought people together. More complex rituals can be done, depending upon the size of the group and the shape of the day. If you are at a workshop, often a ritual around the theme for the day is helpful. At a workshop Reclaiming the Art of Pilgrimage, in New Canaan, Connecticut, we began by standing in a circle around the center of the labyrinth. Each participant walked around the inside of our circle, saying his or her name and "I am a pilgrim seeking . . ." The participants filled in the sentence naming what they sought from the workshop that day.

At Union Seminary in New York we designed a communion service to end the day. While people were walking the labyrinth the ministers stood at the entryway and dedicated the bread and the wine. Prayers were offered as they began following the path to the center. When they met people on the path, they offered them communion. Ritual can be very simple. On Ash Wednesday, we put ashes on our foreheads as we entered the labyrinth. At any time, carrying unlit candles into the center and lighting them for the walk back out into the world is an effective way to symbolize bringing your own light into the world.

Since the labyrinth tapestry has been open daily at Grace, many different groups have come to walk it. Busloads of schoolchildren who planned a tour of the cathedral enjoyed the experience of the winding path. A group of Vietnam veterans came to walk it but would not allow me to present it to them because I represented the church. The parents of a man who recently died of AIDS came back to San Francisco to visit the grieving partner. The three of them came to walk the labyrinth together. They gathered in prayer at the entrance, remembering their lost loved one, and then entered the labyrinth.

Music At Grace Cathedral, a group of vocalists and instrumentalists called Musica Divina comes to chant and play music during the third Wednesday of each month. This evening offers people in the Bay Area an exquisite experience of meditation. Silence supported the Sunday opening of the canvas labyrinth, and this became the preference of many labyrinth walkers. However, during these evenings I became aware of how important music was to me in walking the labyrinth.

During workshops, I began to add music to the experience. At the labyrinth, music can capture the tenor of a group as well as create a climate. Sensing the meditative needs of a group is an art form in itself. Usually the groups of people that come to workshops are hungry for the labyrinth walk. If I sense that they are eager, rather than ambivalent or fearful, I may begin with Hildegard of Bingen's *Feather on the Breath of God*. It is Gregorian chant with modified introductory and ending antiphons. It is usually sung by female voices, which give a modern rather than traditional quality to the experience. I use a variety of modern music as long as it does not have a focused vocal part. Words and story line tend to pull people's attention away from the inner process that the labyrinth encourages. There are exceptions to this. During the Taize around Labyrinth we read the Gospel and chant the prayers, but the people who attend this event know what to expect.

There is a broader dynamic that I am discovering as I see transformations within the labyrinth. I had the privilege of witnessing the planning of the recent Planetary Mass at Grace Cathedral. It was created by a community of Christians from Sheffield, England, and brought to the U.S. through the help of Matthew Fox. This group has combined Christian liturgy with high-tech visuals and modern music in hopes of reaching the youth who feel so stultified by traditional church liturgy. The experience provided a format for me to compare my experience of the visual channel to that of the auditory channel. The eye and the ear are our main intellectual senses, yet they use our intelligence in completely different ways. Taking in data through the eye stimulates the mind and elicits thoughts that connect with feelings. Taking in data through the ear stimulates the imagination and elicits feelings that occur in partnership with thoughts. In the labyrinth workshops the auditory channel is en-

hanced and the visual stimulation is kept at a mini-
mum. The auditory channel is associated with the
right hemisphere of the brain and is able to experience holistic patterns. I believe that auditory stimulation can often enhance the quality of experiences
in the labyrinth, as it did for this man:

> The wonderful music, combined with the walking,
> place me on a high mountaintop in the Himalayas
> with God. I, also, couldn't help but feel how all
> connected we were there on that spiritual path.

THE BIRTH
OF A VISION

The new meaning of soul is creativity and mysticism.
These will become the foundation of the new
psychological type and with him or her
will come the new civilization.

—*Otto Rank*

Gifts from the Labyrinth

Several years ago I was in Anchorage, Alaska, at Saint Mary's Stillpoint Center. My hostess and I drove an hour north into the snow country to meet a group of women who gathered weekly to share their dreams. They had made an eleven-circuit labyrinth lined with stone out in the woods. It was a rugged and hearty labyrinth dotted with small tree trunks here and there and covered with a blanket of fresh snow where no one had yet walked. I was invited to go first, so I began walking unsteadily through the snow. We joyously walked together under a clear blue sky, their dogs barking and running playfully. Soon after I entered the labyrinth, I realized how closely this walk mirrored what was happening with the labyrinth. Each step we took, each footprint in the snow, uncovered and rediscovered the ancient path. And the path, covered by the silent blanket of the many passing seasons over the centuries, was awaiting us.

The labyrinth was designed by an intelligence we cannot fully understand. But this much I do know. The labyrinth is truly a tool for transformation. It is a crucible for change, a blueprint for the sacred meeting of psyche and soul, a field of light, a cosmic dance. It is a center for empowering ritual. It is a container where we can meet angels and recover the great-grandmother's thread, the web of Mary, and the gracious, nurturing God.

Over the years, I have had many special experiences traveling with the labyrinth. I was surprised and delighted to walk the garden labyrinth in Zurich. I was overwhelmed by the four hundred people who came to walk the labyrinth in a park in Austin, Texas. I was awed to enter the labyrinth in the cavernous Chartres Cathedral and thrilled when the permanent labyrinth tapestry arrived at Grace Cathedral. I have come to call these moving and delightful experiences "gifts from the labyrinth."

The labyrinth is gracious and generous with its

gifts for all who enter it. It reintroduces the much-needed walking meditation back into the Christian tradition. It gives the everyday person who may not ordinarily darken the door of church or temple a tool for spiritual experience. It heals and consoles, supports and confronts, and helps us remember the ancient path where others have trod before us. The labyrinth allows us to experience the rhythm of our souls. It weaves us together in the joy and mercy of God's grace.

Many questions remain unanswered. In my notes I came across a sentence that was part of the labyrinth display in Chartres Cathedral in 1993:

*"Messages which in the long run remain
are not understood."*

The labyrinth has many messages for us, and for our times, that remain embedded within its mysterious path, its petals and the lunations, that we have yet to grasp. We do not really know how or why the labyrinth works. I do know that the labyrinth is a profound devotional tool. My hope is that the old masters of the School of Chartres, or whoever birthed the labyrinth into the earthly plane, are pleased that it is being rediscovered. My sense is that they are. I feel gratitude for the enormous amount of help I have been given.

I often describe my experience with the labyrinth as though some mysterious being had snatched me up by the scruff of my neck and carried me out of what was an interesting yet ordinary life. Early on, it placed me in the beauty of Grace Cathedral, with a visionary dean, a vibrant community, and patient colleagues. It gave me friends who were willing to share the adventure. It whisked me away to the dark and mysterious cosmic temple of Chartres Cathedral. It was present with us when we lit candles and said prayers for the Labyrinth Project. It plunked me down amid canvas and paint cans, placed books in my hands and directed across my path people whom I needed to meet. And through this I have learned what it means to live with a grateful heart.

A Vision of
Spiritual Maturity

We need to birth a new vision of what it means to be spiritually mature. Ted Roszak reminded us that we are attempting to develop new human faculties as significant as the discovery of fire or the development of language. The new vision of spiritual maturity is based on a trust of inner wisdom and inner authority that has its moorings in a teaching tradition that guides us in the hard work of soul making.

There is so much we need to attend to in order for our planet to survive. Our loss of connection to the Divine has left us wandering sojourners without clarity of purpose. We have limited ourselves to only one understanding of God, who speaks from outside us, mainly through history. We need to discover that the Holy dwells within and around us. We need to understand that the Scriptures are not simply a book of rules, but a pathway to consciousness. To manifest our creative gifts in this spiritually unimaginative world, we must create from the center of our beings. Wisdom must be evoked from our depths. We need to free ourselves from the shackles of our ancient fears of the imagination to utilize its wisdom.

A new vision allows us to recognize the spark of Divinity within each other, no matter what our race, sex, creed, background, or life-style. Human beings are part of the created order, not above it. Our souls encircle one another. The task is to clear away the hate that lurks in the human mind, so we may join one another to create a workable civilization.

New understandings of ancient knowledge are emerging. Expanded consciousness, the imagination, the mind/body/spirit connections, the use of ritual, the reintroduction of the feminine are all forces that create a new way of understanding humanity's tasks and responsibilities.

Compassion is the core teaching of all the world's spiritual traditions. We must all ask ourselves: Am I growing in compassion? This is the discerning factor. Shared compassion will be the meeting point for our communities. In a spiritually mature world, people will share the richness of their traditions with others from different traditions. Many voices will be heard. As we address the violence in our communities, the drug use, the guns in our schools, we also open up the possibilities of community and cooperation. Many of us hear the drumbeat, the heartthrob of creation. We sense the excitement of rebirth.

It is my responsibility as a spiritual being to clear out the static from my center, to realize my inaccuracies of perception, to rid myself of resentments and insecurities, and to ask for the release of the pebbles in my heart when I am unforgiving. This will allow me to keep focused on the Divine. It is my task, my calling, my responsibility as a human being to find compassion for all forms of life. Through this I am more deeply connected to others and to the web of creation, the source of the thread that guides us and leads us home.

The labyrinth is truly a tool for our times. It can help us find our way through the bewildering multiplicity, to the unity of source. The labyrinth is an evocative experience. The labyrinth provides the sacred space where the inner and outer worlds can commune, where the thinking mind and imaginative heart can flow together. It can provide a space to listen to our inner voice of wisdom and come to grips with our role in humankind's next evolutionary step. Troubled communities can come to the labyrinth to discover and synchronize their vision. It gives us a glimpse of other realms and other ways of knowing.

A Vision of the Labyrinth Project

Awareness of the labyrinth is spreading through the help of many people. I frequently get letters or read newspaper articles on labyrinths being created around the country. I have the sense that the labyrinth is just beginning to make its way into the public stream of consciousness.

We need to restore labyrinths in any way that we can. Many people have created them on their own property. Labyrinths, in their many forms, should be spread across the planet. They should be in cathedrals, parks, conference centers, hospitals, and prisons. Labyrinths should be anywhere we might go in pain, confusion, reverence, or celebration. The labyrinth adds the dimension of the mystical to the everyday ordinary human experience.

The Labyrinth Network based at Grace Cathedral wants to encourage the creation of labyrinths around the country. We hope that leaders will come forth in their communities, form groups, and make labyrinths in whatever form fits the tenor of the community. Labyrinths are lying dormant in almost every world culture. I have not yet seen the ones from Africa, or China, but I have heard of them. Many have been lost but are recorded in out-of-print books. Let's resurrect them. At some point in the near future we will gather at Grace Cathedral to share ideas, learn, and create the next step of this spiritual revolution. Anyone who has worked with a labyrinth knows that it definitely has an agenda of its own. It longs to be out in the world, used by people during this time of spiritual uncertainty.

To close, it is appropriate to once again remember Hildegard of Bingen. Standing in the twelfth century, her light shines in our night sky through her drawings, writings, and music. She brings us a vision of the Sacred through the wisdom figures Sophia, Mother Wisdom, Mother Church. Hildegard knew that the church offered a shortsighted view of the Divine. But she experienced the church as a birthing place for her own creativity, and she recognized that this was the church's true role: to birth the creativity of the people. It is possible to do this through the labyrinth. May we lead a spiritual revolution that includes us all, relies on inner wisdom, accepts the guidance of a wisdom tradition, and recognizes compassion as its guiding principle. Let us allow the Father and Mother God to unite in sacred mystery. Let us build a world community in which all people have the opportunity to create meaning in their own lives. Those who live in poverty, struggle under the burdens of illness and misfortune, those who live as outcasts—all who have no way to lift up their heads to the Divine need the help of others to do so. The Greening Power of God, the Holy Spirit in all Her mystery, is the power of the Divine within. She weaves each of us into the tapestry of this physical life. It is this Power that will bring spiritual transformation to fruition.

The labyrinth is a tool that can connect us to this Power. Long forgotten, sometimes feared, it has been lying dormant in the archives of the Christian mystical tradition under centuries of dust. The creative intelligence that gave us the labyrinth understood the Mystery behind human existence. It bestowed upon us a watering hole for the human spirit, a deep channel for the human soul. The labyrinth is an old watercourse that dried up over time and circumstance. But it is filling again now, with clear, cool waters. It is inviting us to drink. The labyrinth has been awaiting rediscovery, longing to guide us, awaken us while we walk this earthly path. The time has come. I look forward to meeting you by a labyrinth.

AN INVITATION

W here do you plan to be when "the ball drops" in the final moments of the twentieth century? This book is an invitation to a global New Year's Eve party: by then you will be able to find a labyrinth in your area to join the cosmic community that celebrates all life on planet Earth. We will celebrate our pilgrimage to embrace a new vision of spiritual maturity—a maturity that values ethnic, cultural, and gender differences, supports creativity and the work of Spirit among all forms of life. This is what we need for the global family to survive in the twenty-first century.

The Labyrinth
Network
1999!

Grace Cathedral is determined to be a leader in reclaiming the walking meditation as part of the Christian tradition, and to be a source to guide others in the use of the labyrinth as a spiritual tool. We are in the early stages of forming the Labyrinth Network. Our goal is to establish communities of people who gather to use the labyrinth as a central focus on meditation, prayer, group ritual, and transformation.

If you belong to a group that wants to create a labyrinth, or you want to establish one, consider purchasing a seed kit which has explicit instructions on how to design your own labyrinth using the 13-point star to honor the tradition of sacred geometry. We ask that you register your labyrinth, and the names of the original founders of your group, with us so we can direct people to you. And at some point, I would also like to visit your labyrinth. We ask that you share, through our newsletter, rituals, meditations, and experiences, so we may share them with other groups. At times, basic themes would be initiated by Quest/Grace Cathedral—such as creating extended families, healing victims of violence, supporting people facing life-threatening diseases, or developing rites-of-passage rituals for adolescents. This way we would have a spiritual network addressing modern-day issues with a deepening spiritual response. We also hope that you will become part of our data base so that we may contact you in case of a national day of mourning or celebration using the labyrinth, as well as for the New Year's Eve celebration in 1999.

Some groups may also want to develop labyrinths based on other shapes and around numbers other than 13. The hope is that if you choose a different approach, you are intentional about the number that you chose. This way, as part of the network, we could guide people to experiencing different labyrinths.

N o t e s

Chapter One: To Walk a Sacred Path

PAGE

13 *"higher spiritual order"*: J. J. Bachofen, *Mutterrecht und Urreligion,* Leipzig: Kroner, 1926. In Dora M. Kalff's *Sandplay,* Boston: Sigo Press, 1980, p. 31.

15 *"Religion is for those"*: Author unknown.

16 *"I wish I would"*: Karen Armstrong, *The History of God, The Four-Thousand Year Quest of Judaism, Christianity and Islam,* New York: Ballantine Books, 1993, p. xx.

20 *"A single newspaper*: The Path to Enlightenment" by Don Lattin, in the San Francisco Chronicle, December 19, 1991.

21 *"on a spiritual path"*: Thanks to Jean Shinoda Bolen for this clever wording and expanded thought.

22 *"Time is like a necklace"*: Robert Lawlor, *Sacred Geometry, Philosophy and Practice,* London: Thames and Hudson, 1982, p. 24.

Chapter Two: New Pilgrims, New Paths

25 *"centering prayer"*: Thomas Keating, *Open Mind, Open Heart, The Contemplative Dimension of the Gospel,* New York: Amity House, 1986.

27 *"The imagination brings"*: from Iris Murdoch's *The Sovereignty of God.* This book is out of print.

28 "Threefold Path": Saint Teresa of Avila wrote about the Threefold Path in the sixteenth century, much later than when the labyrinth was developed. The Threefold Path does capture a universal process: to

go within, to receive and to go back out into the world, was probably being lived out long before she put words to it.

29 *"Mysticism is the experience"*: Fritjof Capra and David Steindl-Rast, *Belonging to the Universe,* San Francisco: HarperCollins, 1991, p. 56.

33 *"spirit's compass"*: Richard R. Niebuhr, *Pilgrims and Pioneers.*

40 *"not accepted by the ego"*: Wallace B. Clift, *Jung and Christianity: The Challenge of Reconciliation,* New York: Crossroads, 1985, p. 47. This book is an excellent primer for anyone wanting an introduction to C. G. Jung's work.

40 *"the task of"*: Carl Jung, *Modern Man in Search of a Soul,* New York: Harcourt, Brace and World, Inc., 1933.

42 *"Unless we also carry"*: Esther de Waal, *A World Made Whole, Rediscovering the Celtic Tradition,* San Francisco: Fount, (HarperCollins), 1991, p. 56.

Chapter Three: The Labyrinth: Sacred Pattern, Sacred Path

46 *"mandalas"*: *Mandala* is the Sanskrit word that means "circle . . . in the ordinary sense of that word. In the sphere of religious practices and in psychology it denotes circular images, which are drawn, painted, modeled, or danced. Very frequently they contain a quaternity or a multiple of four, in the form of a cross, a star, a square, an octagon, etc." C. G. Jung, *Mandala Symbolism,* translated by R. F. C. Hull, Bollingen Series, Princeton University Press, 1959, p. 3.

46 *"Researchers note"*: *Labyrinths; Solving the Riddle of the Maze,* Adrian Fisher and Georg Gerster, New York: Harmony Books, 1990, p. 12.

47 *"Herodotus"*: Ibid., p. 25.

47 *"any religious practices"*: Jean Favier states: "Many medieval churches have a labyrinth in the nave floor, signifying pilgrimage towards Jerusalem in this world and the road to Salvation in the next world. A symbol of the Christian way, the labyrinth has never really been used for any religious practices." *The World of Chartres,* appendices by John James and Yves Flamand, New York: Abrams, 1988, p. 26. On the other hand, Painton Cowan in *Rose Windows* states: "Labyrinths generally symbolize the path of the soul through life, and medieval pilgrims re-enacted this, following the path of the labyrinth in the cathedral on their knees, symbolizing the journey to Jerusalem." *Rose Windows,* London: Chronicle, Thames and Hudson, 1979, p. 98.

49 *"For the human spirit"*: Robert Lawlor, *Sacred Geometry, Philosophy and Practice,* New York: Thames and Hudson, Inc., 1982, p. 10.

50 *"absolute unity"*: Ibid., p. 23.

50 *"symbolically visible"*: Ibid.

52 *"Sancta Eclesia"*: Fisher and Gerster, op. cit., p. 35.

53 *"Montpelier manuscript"*: Ibid.

53 *"Legend says"*: Louis Charpentier, *The Mysteries of Chartres Cathedral,* Research into Lost Knowledge Organization, 10 Church St. Steeple Bumpstead, Haverhill, Suffolk, translation by Sir Ronald Fraser, 1966.

54 *"a Maltese cross"*: Fisher and Gerster, op. cit., p. 38.

55 *"a whole"*: *Illuminations,* text by Hildegard of Bingen, commentary by Matthew Fox, Santa Fe: Bear and Co., 1985, p. 24.

55 *"When we lift"*: Hugh of St. Victor, a twelfth-century mystic and writer. The source of this quote is unknown.

55 *"Fulbert section"*: Some say that the labyrinth at

Chartres was completed as late as 1230 to 1235. Others surmise that the labyrinth may have been laid in the floor following the completion of the cathedral around 1220. Much of the history of Chartres Cathedral has been lost or destroyed by fire, including dates and the names of the architects. Michael Lampen, Jr., the archivist at Grace Cathedral, noted that the center was sometimes called a lily, also a symbol for the Virgin.

58 *"Venus of classical times"*: Cowan, op. cit., p. 97.

58 *"love beyond passion"*: Ibid.

59 *"before Christian times"*: Ibid., p. 96.

59 *"planetary evolution"*: Keith Critchlow, Jane Carroll, Llewylyn Vaughan Lee, *Chartres Maze, a Model of the Universe?* Research into Lost Knowledge Organization, Occasional Paper No. 1. In this paper he describes the petals as symbols for the six "psychological crises." I have taken the liberty of changing this wording to "evolutionary stages," with Dr. Critchlow's knowledge. This article was originally printed in Architectural Association Quarterly, vol. 5., no. 2, pp. 11–21.

60 *"visit"*: If there are only a few people in the center with me, I can physically move to each petal fairly easily. If there are several people, I move my awareness into each area without moving physically.

60 *"The Lunations"*: This term was not found in any research. Rather, it was created by Richard Feather Anderson and Keith Critchlow in hopes of capturing the lunar essence of this part of the pattern. In an earlier publication, I referred to it as the corona, which is a solar term.

64 *"Grace Cathedral"*: Seed Kits, or instruction kits for the eleven-circuit labyrinth are available by writing The Labyrinth Project, Grace Cathedral, 1051 Taylor Street, San Francisco, CA 94108. These

instruction kits contain the sacred geometry equations, supply list, and organizational approach to make a canvas labyrinth. The equations would apply to other materials as well. The cost is $125, which goes to keeping the Labyrinth Project funded so we can get labyrinths out and around the country. My hope is that a small community of people who have experienced the labyrinth and understand the vision come together, toss money into the pot, and create their own labyrinth to open it to the local community.

64 *"Greek thought"*: My thanks to Michael Lampen, for this information. Evidently Grace Cathedral was designed in the tradition of sacred geometry.

65 *"Mind and Soul"*: Critchlow, et al., op. cit., p. 16.

Chapter Four: Walking the Labyrinth: The Process

82 *"May I Dwell in the Heart"*: Stephen Levine, *Healing into Life and Death,* New York: Doubleday Books, 1987, p. 23.

96 *"guide us along"*: Penelope Reed Doob, *The Idea of the Labyrinth from Classical Antiquity through the Middle Ages,* Ithaca: Cornell University Press, 1990, p. 130.

98 *"with your experience"*: The meditative act does not mean that the walk needs to be slow and serious, however. Labyrinths can be danced, run, and crawled. Sometimes people hug one another as they meet on the path. I encourage people to express the actions that they feel drawn to express.

100 *"Taize Around the Labyrinth"*: This is held every second Friday of the month at Grace Cathedral. Taize is a new form of Christian chanting written by Jacques Berthier for a group of brothers in Taize, France. This form of chant is based on repetitive

phrases so people can easily join in after hearing it once or twice. There is a service format that we have adapted to labyrinth walking.

Chapter Five: The Seeds of Spiritual Hunger

106 *"focused on God"*: Barbara Tuchman, *A Distant Mirror: The Calamitous 14th Century,* New York: Ballantine Books, 1978, p. xix.

106 *"mechanical theory of nature"*: Rupert Sheldrake, *The Rebirth of Nature,* Rochester, Vt.: Park Street Press, 1991, p. 3.

107 *"We live in an age"*: Dora M. Kalff, *Sandplay,* Boston: Sigo Press, 1980. Introduction by Harold Stone, p. 13.

108 *"destroyed or overlaid"*: There is a list of medieval Christian labyrinths from the twelfth to sixteenth centuries in Adrian Fisher and Georg Gerster's *The Art of the Maze,* London: Weidenfeld and Nicolson, 1990, p. 41. This compilation lists both surviving and destroyed labyrinths by location.

108 *"four ways of knowing"*: Jean Favier, *The World of Chartres* appendices by John James and Yves Flamand, New York: Abrams, 1988, pp. 38–41.

109 *"Three central questions"*: Rene Querido, *The Golden Age of Chartres, The Teachings of a Mystery School and the Eternal Feminine,* New York: Floris Books, Anthroposophic Press, 1987, p. 16.

109 *"brilliant masters of Spirit"*: In an earlier pamphlet, I stated that the Labyrinth was possibly part of the Benedictine tradition. This does not seem to be the case.

113 *"a poor nun"*: J. Huizinga, *The Waning of the Middle Ages,* New York: Anchor Books, Doubleday, 1949, reprint 1985, p. 191.

114 *"descended to hell"*: Ibid., p. 193.

114 *"woman in childbirth"*: Ibid., p. 191.

115 *"healthy and vigorous piety"*: Ibid., p. 155.

115 *"burned at the stake"*: Ibid., p. 197.

116 *"words spoken in the imagination"*: Thomas Keating, *Open Mind, Open Heart,* New York: Amity House, 1986, p. 9.

116 *"Angels and devils"*: Ibid., p. 61.

116 *"highest good . . . and deepest evil"*: Kalff, op. cit., from Harold Stone, introduction, p. 19.

117 *"Chartres still denies"*: This is conjecture on my part, but it is informed by the Labyrinth display initiated by Chartres Cathedral in 1993: "In any case, it cannot be a magical place where man pulls hidden forces from the earth. That would be (were one to do so) a perversion of the builders/creators of the labyrinth. For in doing so, one would substitute man in place of God. And God is the ultimate end/final destination of our earthly pilgrimage." The labyrinth may also be closed to the public in an effort to protect a national monument.

117 *"Life of the Spirit"*: Nicholas Berdyaev, *The Meaning of the Creative Act,* New York: Collier Books, 1962, p. 27.

119 *"not the revelation of results"*: Jacob Needleman, *Lost Christianity, A Journey of Rediscovery,* San Francisco: Harper, 1985, p. 96.

120 *"Virgo paritura"*: Favier, op. cit., p. 31.

121 *"black-cloaked old woman"*: Huizinga, op. cit., p. 139. This information comes from the National Film Board of Canada, Part II, *The Burning Times.*

Chapter Six: Rediscovering the Divine Within

129 *"European languages . . . require"*: Robert Lawlor, *Sacred Geometry, Philosophy and Practice,* London: Thames and Hudson, 1982, p. 8.

130 *"Magic Eyes"*: Lewis Smedes, *Forgive and Forget,* San Francisco: HarperCollins, 1991, in the Introduction.

133 *"eating the menu"*: *Reflections on the Art of Living: A Joseph Campbell Companion,* selected by Diane K. Osbon, New York: HarperCollins, 1992, p. 9.

134 *"ways have been charted"*: Andrew Harvey with Mark Matousek, *Dialogues with a Modern Mystic,* Wheaton, Ill.: The Theosophical Publishing House, 1994. p. 41.

136 *"in our hearts"*: Jeremiah 31:31.

139 *"theology of the elect"*: Karen Armstrong, *The History of God, The Four-Thousand-Year Quest of Judaism, Christianity and Islam,* New York: Ballantine Books, 1993, p. 55.

139 *"more brutal God"*: Jeanne Achterberg, *Woman as Healer,* Boston: Shambhala, 1991. Dr. Achterberg made this reference in a lecture presentation.

140 *"immanence recedes"*: James Nelson, *Embodiment,* Minneapolis: Augsberg, Fortress Publishers, 1979. Dr. Nelson made this reference in a lecture presentation.

144 *"sensibilities of the imagination"*: Laurens van der Post, *Jung and the Story of Our Time,* New York: Vintage Books, 1975, p. 21.

Chapter Seven: The Labyrinth: Blueprint for Transformation

150 *"Archetypal images"*: C. G. Jung, *Collected Works,* Bollingen Series, Princeton University Press, vol. 6: 183, p. 39.

150 *"creative fantasy"*: C. G. Jung, "The Spirit of Man, Art and Literature," *Collected Works*, vol. 5, par. 127.

151 *"Christ as perfect"*: Ibid. Jung, *Collected Works*, vol. 9, 1, p. 215.

152 *"the Self"*: Wallace B. Cliff, *Jung and Christianity, The Challenge of Reconciliation*, New York: Crossroads, 1985, p. 22. Cliff also refers us to Jung's *Aion*, subtitled "Researches into the Phenomenology of the Self," *Collected Works*, vol. 9, 2, pp. 22–35.

152 *"chords were struck"*: Ibid. Jung, *Collected Works*, vol. 5, par. 128.

152 *"Archetypes are like riverbeds"*: Carl Jung, *Psychological Reflections, A New Anthology of His Writings 1905–1961*, edited by Joland Jacobi and R. F. C. Hull, Bollingen Series, Princeton University Press, 1973. Quote from 115:395, *Collected Works*.

154 *"you must have a room"*: Joseph Campbell, *The Power of Myth*, Doubleday: New York, 1988. p. 38.

156 *"moment of illumination"*: Michael Samuels, M.D., and Nancy Samuels, *Seeing with the Mind's Eye: The History, Techniques and Uses of Visualization*, New York: Random House and Bookworks, 1975, p. 259.

162 *"understanding the spider"*: Andrew Harvey, with Mark Matousek, *Dialogues with a Modern Mystic*, Wheaton, Ill.: Theosophical Publishing House, 1994, p. 28.

163 *"children of God"*: Matthew 5:3–9.

164 *"pharmacist of bliss"*: Harvey, op. cit., pp. 122–123.

167 *"by their fruits"*: Matthew 7:16.

171 *"I am a pilgrim"*: Sarah Epperly of New Paths through Ritual designed this effective opening in the New Canaan, Connecticut, workshop.

173 *"Feather on the Breath"*: The Narada label offers good labyrinth music. Nancy Rumble and Eric Tin-

dahl's works *Homeland,* and *Legends* are two that I use frequently. The Labyrinth Project of New Canaan introduced me to David Darling's *Eight String Religion*. The Native American Flute player R. Carlos Nakai has several albums out. I use *Carrying the Gift* with William Eaton.

Chapter Eight: The Birth of a Vision

180 *"many people"*: I want to acknowledge and thank Keith Critchlow, Richard Feather Anderson, Angeles Arrien, Joanna Macy, Carla de Sola, Joan McMillan, Alex Champion, Susan Alexjander, Barbara Cavanaugh, Jan Chastian, Alayne Longfellow Heinle, Richard Russell, Sally Ackerly, for their help in launching the labyrinth. Helen Curry, for her courage in launching The Labyrinth Project of New Canaan, Connecticut, and Nancy Millner and Bill Arnold for their grace-filled leadership of the Chrysalis Group in Richmond, Virginia. Many others are setting up Labyrinth Projects in their area at the time of this writing.

182 *"Mother Church"*: *Illuminations,* text by Hildegard of Bingen, commentary by Matthew Fox, Santa Fe: Bear and Co., 1985, p. 71.

R e s o u r c e s

Basic Books on Labyrinths:

Janet Bord, *Mazes and Labyrinths of the World,* London: Latimer Press, 1976.

Alex Champion, *Earth Mazes,* Earth Mazes Publishing, P.O. Box 145, Philo, CA 95466. An American builder of mazes and labyrinths.

Penelope Reed Doob, *The Idea of the Labyrinth from Classical Antiquity through the Middle Ages,* Ithaca: Cornell University Press, 1990.

Adrian Fisher, *Labyrinths: Solving the Riddle of the Maze,* New York: Harmony Books, 1991. This book was reprinted under the title *The Art of the Maze,* London: Weidenfeld and Nicolson, 1990.

Herman Kern, *Labyrinthe,* München: Prestel-Verlas, 1982. This book is in German only.

Richard Lawlor, *Sacred Geometry, Philosophy and Practice,* London: Thames and Hudson Ltd, 1982.

Sig Lonegren, *Labyrinths, Ancient Myths and Modern Uses,* Gothic Image Publications, 7 High Street, Glastonbury, Somerset BA6 9DP, England, 1991.

W. H. Matthews, *Mazes and Labyrinths, Their History and Development,* New York: Dover Publications, 1970.

Jill Purce, *The Mystic Spiral, Journey of the Soul,* New York: Norton, 1974.

Rene Querido, *The Golden Age of Chartres, The Teachings of a Mystery School and the Eternal Feminine,* New York: Floris Books, Anthroposophic Press, 1987.

Tapes, Magazines, and Other Resources

Richard Feather Anderson, *Geomancer's Booksource,* an
annotated bibliography, resource guide, and mail order
service of books recommended by Richard Feather
Anderson. 7310 Bodega Avenue, Sebastopol, CA
95472. Phone 707-829-8413.

Richard Feather Anderson, *Labyrinths: A-Mazing Paths
to Wholeness.* This lecture tape covers the origins,
common elements, and different types of labyrinths;
the beneficial effects of traversing; their functions as
metaphors as well as physical pathways for the transformative journey. Taped at the American Society of
Dowsers in Danville, Vermont, September, 1988.
Available in audio or video.

Richard Feather Anderson, *Labyrinths: Clues to the Mystery of Life.* A lecture on universal patterns of life en-
coded within the seven-circuit Cretan Labyrinth and
the Chartres Cathedral Laybrinth. Available in video.
Richard Feather Anderson is also available for design
consultation and direction.

Caerdroia Magazine, edited by Jeff and Deb Saward. A
journal that connects labyrinth enthusiasts worldwide,
presenting their ideas, research, and activities. Published annually at year end. Subscription also includes
a small newsletter published annually at midsummer.
$15/year subscription: 53 Thundersley Grove, Thun-
dersley, Benfleet, Essex SS7 3EB, England. Phone
0268-751915.

Music:

"Remembering the Way." Music by Joan McMillan of
Menlo Park, CA.

On Chartres Cathedral

Henry Adams, *Mont Saint Michel and Chartres*, New York: Penguin Books, 1986.

Painton Cowan, *Rose Windows*, London: Chronicle, Thames and Hudson, 1979.

Jean Favier, *The World of Chartres*, appendices by John James and Yves Flamand, New York: Abrams, 1988.

John James, *The Master Masons of Chartres*, London: West Grinstead, 1990.

Colin Ward, *Chartres, The Making of a Miracle*, London: The Folio Society, 1986.

Other Resources:

Jeanne Achterberg, *Woman as Healer*, Boston: Shambhala, 1991.

Karen Armstrong, *The History of God, The Four-Thousand-Year Quest of Judaism, Christianity and Islam*, New York: Ballantine Books, 1993.

Susan Gablik, *The Reenchantment of Art*, New York: Thames and Hudson, 1991.

J. Huizinga, *The Waning of the Middle Ages*, New York: Anchor Books, Doubleday, 1949.

Illuminations, text by Hildegard of Bingen, commentary by Matthew Fox, Santa Fe: Bear and Co., 1985.

Dora M. Kalff, *Sandplay*, Boston: Sigo Press, 1980.

Thomas Keating, *Open Mind, Open Heart*, New York: Amity House, 1986.

Jacob Needleman, *Lost Christianity, A Journey of Rediscovery*, San Fancisco: Harper, 1985.

Esther de Waal, *A World Made Whole, Rediscovering the Celtic Tradition*, San Francisco: Fount (Harper-Collins), 1991. This book was reprinted under the new title *Every Earthly Blessing, Celebrating a Spirituality of Creation*, Ann Arbor: Servant, 1992.

The **Reverend Dr. Lauren Artress** is Canon for Special Ministries at San Francisco's Grace Cathedral. She is also the founder of Quest: Grace Cathedral Center for Spiritual Wholeness and the creator of the Labyrinth Project. In keeping with Quest's vision of addressing the spiritual hunger of our times, she lectures and leads Labyrinth workshops nationwide. Dr. Artress earned her master's degree in religious education from Princeton Theological Seminary and her doctor of ministry degree from Andover Newton Theological School, and received her analytic training at the Blanton Peale Graduate Institute. A licensed psychotherapist in the state of California, she lives in San Francisco.